D MATHEMATICS
Skills, Concepts, Problem Solving

Illustrations: Pages 36, 98 (spring), 100: Marty Husted; Pages 47, 49, 59, 77, 93 (winter, beach), 98 (winter, fall, summer), 110 (paper), 113, 114, 119: Laurie Conley; Page 67: Margaret Lindmark; Page 92 (turkey, man): Matt LeBarre; Page 110 (shoebox, can, golf ball, ice cubes): Zeke Smith

Photo Credits: Front Cover: Corbis/Punchstock; Page 4: www.shutterstock.com, Andrey Parfyonov; Page 9: www.shutterstock.com, Kevin R Williams; Page 12: www.shutterstock.com, Tomasz Trojanowski; Page 17: www.shutterstock.com, Apollofoto; Page 21: www.shutterstock.com, Ramon Berk; Page 26: www.shutterstock.com, Cherick; Page 32: www.shutterstock.com, Katrina Brown; Page 34: www.shutterstock.com, paulaphoto; Page 35: www.shutterstock.com, Graca Victoria; Page 42: www.shutterstock.com, Uwe Bumann; Page 43: www.shutterstock.com, Michael Zysman; Page 44: www.shutterstock.com, Racheal Grazias; Page 56: www.istockphoto.com/steps; Page 62 (top): www.shutterstock.com, egd; (bottom) www.shutterstock.com, Richard Thornton; Page 69: www.istockphoto.com/joanek; Page 78 (top): www.shutterstock.com, Jeff R. Clow; (bottom): www.shutterstock.com, Cheryl Casey; Page 81: www.shutterstock.com, Brian Daly; Page 86: www.shutterstock.com, Ferenc Szelepcsenyi; Page 88: www.shutterstock.com, Galyna Andrushko; Page 94: www.shutterstock.com, Mikulich Alexander Andreevich; Page 96: www.shutterstock.com, semenovp; Page 117: www.shutterstock.com, Heidi Hart; Page 118: www.shutterstock.com, Nicole Gordine; Page 120: www.shutterstock.com, rashad

ISBN 978-0-8454-5860-0

Copyright © 2009 The Continental Press, Inc.

No part of this publication may be reproduced in any form or by any means, electronic, mechanical, photocopying, recording, or otherwise, without the prior written permission of the publisher. All rights reserved. Printed in the United States of America.

Continental Press

Contents

- 3 ..... Addition: Facts to 18
- 4 ..... Adding Three or Four Numbers
- 5 ..... Missing Addends
- 6 ..... Subtraction: Facts to 18
- 7 ..... Subtraction, the Inverse of Addition
- 8 ..... Addition and Subtraction Practice
- 9 ..... Problem Solving: Choosing the Operation
- 10 ..... Place Value: Hundreds, Tens, and Ones
- 11 ..... Ordering and Comparing Numbers
- 12 ..... Rounding Numbers
- 13 ..... Money: Dollars and Cents
- 14 ..... Place Value: Thousands
- 15 ..... Comparing and Ordering Large Numbers
- 16 ..... Place Value: Millions
- 17 ..... Problem Solving: Using a Pictograph
- 18 ..... Adding Two-Digit Numbers
- 19 ..... Adding Three-Digit Numbers
- 20 ..... Adding Four-Digit Numbers
- 21 ..... Problem Solving: Identifying Extra Information
- 22 ..... Subtracting Two-Digit Numbers
- 23 ..... Subtracting Three-Digit Numbers
- 24 ..... Subtracting Across Zeros
- 25 ..... Subtracting Four-Digit Numbers
- 26 ..... Problem Solving: Identifying Insufficient Information
- 27 ..... Estimating Sums and Differences
- 28 ..... Checking Addition and Subtraction
- 29 ..... Adding and Subtracting Large Numbers
- 30 ..... Problem Solving: Finding Missing Information
- 31 ..... Multiplying 2s and 3s
- 32 ..... Multiplying 4s and 5s
- 33 ..... Properties of Multiplication
- 34 ..... Multiplying 6s and 7s
- 35 ..... Mutliplying 8s and 9s
- 36 ..... Problem Solving: Writing a Number Sentence
- 37 ..... Finding Multiples
- 38 ..... Multiplication and Missing Factors
- 39 ..... Dividing by 2 and 3
- 40 ..... Dividing by 4 and 5
- 41 ..... Division, the Inverse of Multiplication
- 42 ..... Dividing by 6 and 7
- 43 ..... Dividing by 8 and 9
- 44 ..... Problem Solving: Planning Two-Step Solutions
- 45 ..... Finding Factors
- 46 ..... Division with Remainders
- 47 ..... Problem Solving: Interpreting a Remainder
- 48 ..... Time: Hours and Minutes
- 49 ..... Problem Solving: Finding Elapsed Time
- 50 ..... Problem Solving: Using Units of Time
- 51 ..... Money
- 52 ..... Making Change
- 53 ..... Extending Multiplication: Multiples of 10 and 100
- 54 ..... Multiplying Two-Digit Numbers
- 55 ..... Multiplying Three- and Four-Digit Numbers
- 56 ..... Problem Solving: Using a Bar Graph
- 57 ..... Dividing Two- and Three-Digit Numbers
- 58 ..... Dividing Three- and Four-Digit Numbers
- 59 ..... Problem Solving: Finding Averages
- 60 ..... Estimating Products and Quotients
- 61 ..... Order of Operations
- 62 ..... Problem Solving: Using the Four Operations
- 63 ..... Fractions: Parts of a Whole
- 64 ..... Fractions: Parts of a Set
- 65 ..... Finding a Fraction of a Set
- 66 ..... Equivalent Fractions
- 67 ..... Equivalent Fractions in Higher Terms
- 68 ..... Equivalent Fractions in Lower Terms
- 69 ..... Problem Solving: Using a Circle Graph
- 70 ..... Mixed Numbers
- 71 ..... Changing Fractions to Mixed Numbers
- 72 ..... Comparing Fractions and Mixed Numbers
- 73 ..... Adding Fractions with Like Denominators
- 74 ..... Subtracting Fractions with Like Denominators
- 75 ..... Adding Fractions with Unlike Denominators
- 76 ..... Subtracting Fractions with Unlike Denominators
- 77 ..... Adding and Subtracting Mixed Numbers
- 78 ..... Problem Solving: Using Fractions and Mixed Numbers
- 79 ..... Ratios
- 80 ..... Probability
- 81 ..... Problem Solving: Making a Tree Diagram
- 82 ..... Decimals: Tenths
- 83 ..... Decimals: Hundredths
- 84 ..... Comparing and Ordering Decimals
- 85 ..... Adding Decimals
- 86 ..... Subtracting Decimals
- 87 ..... Adding and Subtracting Decimals
- 88 ..... Problem Solving: Using Decimals
- 89 ..... Measurement: Centimeter
- 90 ..... Measurement: Metric Units of Length
- 91 ..... Measurement: Mililiter and Liter
- 92 ..... Measurement: Gram and Kilogram
- 93 ..... Measurement: Degrees Celsius
- 94 ..... Problem Solving: Using Hidden Information
- 95 ..... Measurement: Inch, Half Inch, Quarter Inch
- 96 ..... Measurement: Customary Units of Length
- 97 ..... Measurement: Customary Units of Capacity and Weight
- 98 ..... Measurement: Degrees Fahrenheit
- 99 ..... Problem Solving: Using a Line Graph
- 100 ..... Problem Solving: Making a Table
- 101 ..... Geometry: Lines and Line Segments
- 102 ..... Geometry: Rays and Angles
- 103 ..... Geometry: Polygons
- 104 ..... Geometry: Circles
- 105 ..... Geometry: Congruence and Similarity
- 106 ..... Geometry: Symmetry
- 107 ..... Geometry: Ordered Pairs
- 108 ..... Geometry: Perimeter
- 109 ..... Geometry: Area
- 110 ..... Geometry: Solid Figures
- 111 ..... Geometry: Volume
- 112 ..... Problem Solving: Drawing a Picture
- 113 ..... Multiplying by Tens
- 114 ..... Multiplying by Two-Digit Numbers
- 115 ..... Multiplying by Two-Digit Numbers
- 116 ..... Dividing by Tens
- 117 ..... Dividing by Two-Digit Numbers
- 118 ..... Dividing by Two-Digit Numbers
- 119 ..... Problem Solving: Using Rates
- 120 ..... Problem Solving: Guessing and Checking

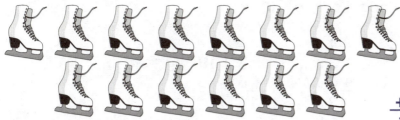

8 skates
+6 skates
14 skates

Addends
8 + 6 = 14
Sum

Add.

1. 3
  +3

2. 1
  +4

3. 2
  +6

4. 7
  +0

5. 4
  +5

6. 9
  +1

7. 4
  +3

8. 5
  +5

9. 9
  +2

10. 8
  +4

11. 3
  +7

12. 4
  +4

13. 0
  +5

14. 3
  +6

15. 7
  +7

16. 5
  +3

17. 8
  +6

18. 7
  +4

19. 7
  +8

20. 8
  +7

21. 9
  +3

22. 4
  +8

23. 6
  +5

24. 5
  +6

25. 6 + 6 = _____
26. 8 + 5 = _____
27. 4 + 9 = _____
28. 9 + 8 = _____

29. 7 + 6 = _____
30. 9 + 9 = _____
31. 5 + 7 = _____
32. 6 + 4 = _____

33. 9 + 5 = _____
34. 3 + 8 = _____
35. 8 + 8 = _____
36. 0 + 0 = _____

37. 9 + 7 = _____
38. 6 + 9 = _____
39. 6 + 7 = _____
40. 8 + 2 = _____

41. A group of 7 girls and 3 boys went ice-skating. How many people went skating in all?

42. Jordan went skating 8 times in January and 9 times in February. How many times did he go in all?

Addition: Facts to 18

You can group numbers in any way to add. Look for 10.

$$\begin{array}{r}4\\3\\+6\\\hline13\end{array}\Big)7 \qquad \begin{array}{r}4\\3\\+6\\\hline13\end{array}\Big)9 \qquad \begin{array}{r}4\\3\\+6\\\hline13\end{array}\Big)10$$

Add. Look for 10.

1. 2, 8, +5
2. 1, 5, +5
3. 6, 0, +4
4. 5, 4, +5
5. 6, 7, +3
6. 8, 9, +1

7. 2, 4, +6
8. 2, 5, +3
9. 1, 9, +8
10. 8, 6, +2
11. 4, 7, +2
12. 3, 6, +7

13. 6, 2, 4, +3
14. 3, 2, 2, +2
15. 1, 3, 7, +7
16. 4, 1, 0, +9
17. 5, 9, 2, +1
18. 6, 8, 0, +2

Solve each problem below. Then find the letter that matches each sum. Write it in the box to solve the riddle.

What do you call a cat that eats lemons?

CODE
13 = P
14 = O
15 = R
16 = U
18 = S

19. 5 + 9 + 0 + 4 = ____
20. 6 + 1 + 4 + 3 = ____
21. 5 + 0 + 3 + 8 = ____
22. 7 + 2 + 4 + 2 = ____
23. 0 + 8 + 2 + 3 = ____
24. 4 + 3 + 7 + 2 = ____
25. 2 + 3 + 4 + 9 = ____
26. 5 + 5 + 4 + 4 = ____

Adding Three or Four Numbers

Fill in each box.

1. 5 + ☐ = 10
2. 8 + ☐ = 12
3. 4 + ☐ = 11
4. 9 + ☐ = 15

5. 1 + ☐ = 10
6. 9 + ☐ = 17
7. 7 + ☐ = 13
8. 6 + ☐ = 14

9. ☐ + 5 = 14
10. ☐ + 9 = 16
11. ☐ + 3 = 11
12. ☐ + 8 = 13

13. ☐ + 9 = 18
14. ☐ + 4 = 10
15. ☐ + 5 = 12
16. ☐ + 7 = 14

17. 7 + ☐ = 10
18. 2 + ☐ = 11
19. ☐ + 8 = 16

20. ☐ + 6 = 11
21. 8 + ☐ = 15
22. ☐ + 9 = 13

23. 6 + ☐ = 14
24. ☐ + 9 = 17
25. 9 + ☐ = 18

26. ☐ + 7 + 3 = 11
27. 6 + ☐ + 8 = 14
28. 5 + 4 + ☐ = 16

29. 8 + ☐ + 6 = 17
30. 9 + 0 + ☐ = 13
31. ☐ + 1 + 5 = 15

32. 2 + 5 + ☐ = 12
33. ☐ + 3 + 6 = 18
34. 0 + ☐ + 9 = 10

Missing Addends

5

$$\begin{array}{r}7\text{ bats}\\-3\text{ bats}\\\hline 4\text{ bats}\end{array}\qquad 7-3=4$$

Difference

Subtract.

1. $9 - 1$
2. $7 - 0$
3. $14 - 8$
4. $11 - 6$
5. $10 - 2$
6. $11 - 5$

7. $10 - 7$
8. $14 - 6$
9. $12 - 5$
10. $9 - 9$
11. $13 - 4$
12. $15 - 6$

13. $16 - 7$
14. $13 - 9$
15. $9 - 3$
16. $12 - 9$
17. $8 - 6$
18. $11 - 7$

19. $12 - 7$
20. $11 - 4$
21. $10 - 6$
22. $16 - 8$
23. $13 - 6$
24. $18 - 9$

25. $11 - 2 =$ ____
26. $14 - 7 =$ ____
27. $13 - 5 =$ ____
28. $12 - 6 =$ ____

29. $15 - 9 =$ ____
30. $17 - 8 =$ ____
31. $0 - 0 =$ ____
32. $11 - 3 =$ ____

33. $12 - 4 =$ ____
34. $13 - 7 =$ ____
35. $16 - 9 =$ ____
36. $14 - 5 =$ ____

37. $8 - 3 =$ ____
38. $10 - 5 =$ ____
39. $15 - 7 =$ ____
40. $11 - 9 =$ ____

41. Phyllis knows 12 monster jokes. She told Thomas 3 of them. How many more does Phyllis have to tell?

42. Carmen got 13 candy bars while trick-or-treating. She ate 8 of them. How many does she have left?

Subtraction: Facts to 18

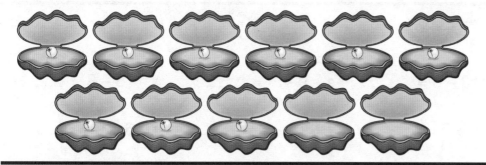

Think:

```
  11        9
-  9      + 2
———       ———
   2       11
```

Subtract by finding the missing addend.

1. 12   2. 14   3. 11   4. 17   5. 13   6. 15
   − 4   − 9   − 5   − 8   − 6   − 7

7. 13   8. 11   9. 16   10. 12   11. 14   12. 18
   − 4   − 3   − 9   − 7   − 8   − 9

13. 17   14. 15   15. 12   16. 13   17. 12   18. 15
   − 9   − 6   − 8   − 5   − 3   − 8

19. 13   20. 11   21. 14   22. 10   23. 16   24. 12
   − 8   − 7   − 5   − 4   − 8   − 5

Write two addition and two subtraction problems for each group of numbers.

25. **6, 7, 13**

```
   6      13       7
 +7       −—     +—      −6
———      ———    ———    ———
  13       6
```

26. **4, 8, 12**

27. **7, 9, 16**

Subtraction, the Inverse of Addition

Add or subtract. Watch the signs.

1. 5 + 7 = ___
2. 13 − 6 = ___
3. 9 + 5 = ___
4. 16 − 8 = ___
5. 11 − 8 = ___
6. 8 + 7 = ___
7. 14 − 6 = ___
8. 6 + 9 = ___
9. 6 + 5 = ___
10. 12 − 4 = ___
11. 7 + 7 = ___
12. 18 − 9 = ___
13. 15 − 6 = ___
14. 5 + 8 = ___
15. 17 − 8 = ___
16. 7 + 9 = ___

Complete.

17. 13 − ☐ = 4
18. ☐ − 9 = 8
19. ☐ + 7 = 11
20. ☐ − 6 = 8
21. 11 − ☐ = 5
22. ☐ + 5 = 13
23. ☐ + 9 = 11
24. ☐ − 6 = 9
25. 8 + ☐ = 16
26. 12 − ☐ = 5
27. ☐ + 9 = 18
28. 9 + ☐ = 17
29. 6 + 8 = ☐ + 7
    ___ = ☐ + 7
30. ☐ − 6 = 14 − 5
    ☐ − 6 = ___
31. 5 + ☐ = 17 − 8
    5 + ☐ = ___
32. ☐ − 5 = 13 − 6
    ☐ − 5 = ___
33. 14 − 9 = ☐ + 3
    ___ = ☐ + 3
34. 4 + 8 = 6 + ☐
    ___ = 6 + ☐

Addition and Subtraction Practice

Use these four steps to find answers to the problems below.

Step 1. **Read** the problem carefully.
Step 2. **Think:** What do I know?
   What must I find out?
   How can I find the answer?
     Circle *add* or *subtract*.
Step 3. **Solve.** Write the problem and find the answer.
Step 4. **Check** the answer. Does it make sense?

---

1. Jerome entered 12 hens in the fair. Of these, 4 of them won ribbons. How many did not win?

   add   subtract

2. Ms. Aviles won 7 first prizes, 4 second prizes, and 3 third prizes. How many prizes did she win?

   add   subtract

3. Steven drove 3 miles to Bellton and then 8 more miles to the fair. How far did he drive in all?

   add   subtract

4. Mrs. Dinh judged 13 cakes. She gave prizes to 6 of them. How many cakes did not get prizes?

   add   subtract

5. There are 6 judges for animals and 9 judges for other things. How many judges are there in all?

   add   subtract

6. Harry won 7 ribbons. His sister won 5. How many did they win altogether?

   add   subtract

7. Byron has 11 perfect ears of corn. That's 3 more than he needs to enter. How many does he need?

   add   subtract

8. Zenaida entered 9 cows in the fair and 4 won prizes. How many did not win prizes?

   add   subtract

Problem Solving: Choosing the Operation

Write each number in standard form.

1. sixteen   _16_
2. eighty-three   ____
3. thirty-four   ____
4. seventy-nine   ____
5. sixty-five   ____
6. forty   ____
7. six hundred fifty-two   ____
8. eight hundred eighty-four   ____
9. two hundred seventy   ____
10. seven hundred twenty-one   ____
11. five hundred nine   ____
12. four hundred ninety-eight   ____
13. one hundred six   ____
14. three hundred thirteen   ____

Write each number name.

15. 46   _forty-six_
16. 24   ____
17. 81   ____
18. 39   ____
19. 325   ____
20. 672   ____
21. 569   ____
22. 854   ____
23. 290   ____
24. 117   ____

Write each number in expanded form.

25. 345 = _300 + 40 + 5_
26. 903 = ____
27. 28 = ____
28. 72 = ____
29. 680 = ____
30. 59 = ____
31. 896 = ____
32. 408 = ____

Place Value: Hundreds, Tens, and Ones

Write the numbers that come just before and just after.

1. ___ 32 ___
2. ___ 48 ___
3. ___ 259 ___
4. ___ 19 ___
5. ___ 71 ___
6. ___ 820 ___
7. ___ 50 ___
8. ___ 89 ___
9. ___ 340 ___
10. ___ 99 ___
11. ___ 60 ___
12. ___ 167 ___

The symbol > means *is greater than*. The symbol < means *is less than*.

$$50 > 49 \qquad 17 < 19$$

Write > or < in each circle.

13. 64 ◯ 65
14. 185 ◯ 184
15. 645 ◯ 654
16. 42 ◯ 32
17. 702 ◯ 603
18. 860 ◯ 859
19. 38 ◯ 47
20. 381 ◯ 391
21. 502 ◯ 487
22. 80 ◯ 79
23. 909 ◯ 910
24. 236 ◯ 263

Write a number sentence to compare the weights of each pair of animals.

ANIMAL WEIGHTS

Animal	Pounds
bear	278
beaver	54
deer	152
eagle	13
fox	12
lion	367
owl	16
tiger	376
wolf	125

25. beaver / bear

___ ◯ ___

26. wolf / lion

___ ◯ ___

27. fox / owl

___ ◯ ___

28. beaver / fox

___ ◯ ___

29. deer / wolf

___ ◯ ___

30. eagle / owl

___ ◯ ___

31. lion / tiger

___ ◯ ___

32. bear / tiger

___ ◯ ___

Ordering and Comparing Numbers

Round a number to the nearest **ten** by looking at the **ones**.
28 is between 20 and 30. It is closer to 30.
Round 28 **up** to 30.

75 is halfway between 70 and 80. Round 75 **up** to 80.

143 is between 140 and 150. It is closer to 140.
Round 143 **down** to 140.

Round each number to the nearest ten.

1. 24 _____
2. 37 _____
3. 52 _____
4. 61 _____
5. 89 _____
6. 793 _____
7. 629 _____
8. 73 _____
9. 455 _____
10. 384 _____
11. 902 _____
12. 197 _____

Round a number to the nearest **hundred** by looking at the **tens**.
425 is between 400 and 500. It is closer to 400.
Round 425 **down** to 400.

150 is halfway between 100 and 200. Round 150 **up** to 200.

872 is between 800 and 900. It is closer to 900.
Round 872 **up** to 900.

Round each number to the nearest hundred.

13. 184 _____
14. 349 _____
15. 850 _____
16. 208 _____
17. 255 _____
18. 691 _____
19. 745 _____
20. 565 _____
21. 146 _____
22. 832 _____
23. 487 _____
24. 924 _____

25. Detective Eye has solved 438 cases. Round the number of cases he has solved to the—

    nearest ten _____

    nearest hundred _____

26. Detective Eye found 152 fingerprints on a safe. Round the number of fingerprints he found to the—

    nearest ten _____

    nearest hundred _____

Rounding Numbers

The Treat Shop

Steak Sandwich	**$3.89**
Cheese Steak	**$4.25**
Deluxe Hamburger	**$3.47**
Fried Chicken	**$5.68**
French Fries	**$0.96**
Milk Shake	**$1.74**

Find each price in the menu above. Then write each amount.

1. steak sandwich _____ dollars and _____ cents or $_____ . _____
2. french fries _____ dollars and _____ cents or _____
3. fried chicken _____ dollars and _____ cents or _____
4. cheese steak _____ dollars and _____ cents or _____
5. milk shake _____ dollar and _____ cents or _____
6. deluxe hamburger _____ dollars and _____ cents or _____

Write each amount using a $ and a decimal point.

7. 79 cents _____
8. 8 dollars _____
9. 2 dollars and 30 cents _____
10. 7 dollars and 9 cents _____
11. 1 dollar and 14 cents _____
12. 9 dollars and 35 cents _____
13. 56 cents _____
14. 4 dollars and 29 cents _____
15. 5 cents _____
16. 5 dollars and 73 cents _____
17. 7 dollars _____
18. 3 dollars and 98 cents _____

Round each amount to the nearest ten cents.

19. $9.21 _____
20. $0.47 _____
21. $2.05 _____
22. $8.99 _____
23. $5.44 _____
24. $6.72 _____

Round each amount to the nearest dollar.

25. $0.75 _____
26. $6.50 _____
27. $4.49 _____
28. $8.39 _____
29. $9.15 _____
30. $7.52 _____

Money: Dollars and Cents

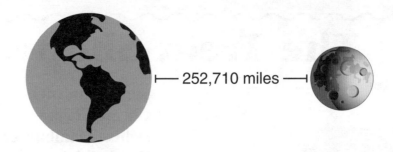

The moon is two hundred fifty-two thousand, seven hundred ten miles from Earth.

Write each number in expanded form.

1. 6,245 = 6,000 + 200 + 40 + 5
2. 47,890 = _____
3. 2,609 = _____
4. 592,784 = _____
5. 30,927 = _____
6. 803,075 = _____

Write each number in standard form.

7. one thousand, eight hundred forty-nine _____
8. fifteen thousand, four hundred eight _____
9. three thousand, seventy-one _____
10. seventy-two thousand, five hundred ninety-six _____
11. nine hundred six thousand, one hundred _____
12. eight hundred twenty-nine thousand, two hundred seventy _____

Write the total value of the underlined digit.

13. <u>2</u>9,607   20,000
14. 5,<u>8</u>34 _____
15. <u>6</u>18,500 _____
16. <u>9</u>,015 _____
17. 8<u>2</u>,432 _____
18. <u>2</u>00,036 _____

19. <u>4</u>,723 _____
20. <u>9</u>2,040 _____
21. <u>1</u>00,086 _____
22. 1,0<u>3</u>1 _____
23. 36,42<u>8</u> _____
24. 70<u>4</u>,670 _____

14

Place Value: Thousands

Write the number that is—

1 more than:
1. 8,325 _____
2. 4,699 _____

10 more than:
3. 7,894 _____
4. 33,002 _____

100 more than:
5. 40,216 _____
6. 129,941 _____

1 less than:
7. 40,000 _____
8. 2,650 _____

100 less than:
9. 5,012 _____
10. 18,407 _____

1,000 less than:
11. 80,649 _____
12. 711,003 _____

Complete.

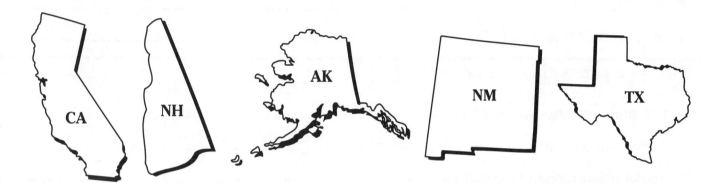

13. The five states listed below are the smallest in the United States. Write the names of the states in the blanks in order of size, beginning with the smallest.

Connecticut	5,543 square miles	_____
Delaware	2,489 square miles	_____
New Hampshire	9,350 square miles	_____
New Jersey	8,721 square miles	_____
Rhode Island	1,545 square miles	_____

14. The five states listed below are the largest in the United States. Write the names of the states in the blanks in order of size, beginning with the largest.

Alaska	663,267 square miles	_____
California	163,696 square miles	_____
Montana	147,042 square miles	_____
New Mexico	121,589 square miles	_____
Texas	268,581 square miles	_____

Comparing and Ordering Large Numbers

275,800,401 results

two hundred seventy-five million, eight hundred thousand, four hundred one search results

Write each number in expanded form.

1. 500,200,010 = _____
2. 72,581,990 = _____
3. 108,020,600 = _____
4. 827,009,005 = _____

Write each number in standard form.

5. five hundred fifty-two million _____
6. twenty million, four hundred thousand, sixty _____
7. seven million, eight hundred thirty-one _____
8. sixty-three million, twelve thousand, nine _____

The table below lists the cities in the United States with the largest populations. Write the names of the cities in order from largest to smallest. Then answer the questions.

POPULATIONS OF CITIES

City	Population
Chicago	2,836,658
Houston	2,208,180
Los Angeles	3,834,340
New York City	8,274,527
Phoenix	1,552,259

9. _____
_____
_____
_____
_____

10. Which is larger, Houston or Phoenix? _____
11. Which is smaller, Chicago or Los Angeles? _____
12. Which city has more than five million people? _____
13. Which city has fewer than two million people? _____
14. Which city is the smallest? _____
15. Which city is the largest? _____

Place Value: Millions

Use the pictograph to answer each question.

THIS MONTH'S SALES AT COMPU-GAME HOUSE	◎ = 100 games
Space Trek	◎ ◎ ◎ ◎ ◎ ◎
Bright Knights	◎ ◎ ◎ ◎ ◎
Barium Brothers	◎ ◎ ◎ ◎ ◎ ◎ ◎ ◎
Tanks Ahoy!	◎ ◎ ◖
El Kid	◎ ◎ ◎ ◎ ◎ ◎ ◎ ◎ ◎ ◎ ◖
Down the Tubes	◎ ◎ ◎ ◎ ◎
Giant Hamsters	◎ ◎ ◎ ◎ ◎ ◎ ◎ ◖
Lakes & Snaggles	◎

1. What does this pictograph show? _____
   _____
2. How many games does one ◎ stand for? _____
3. How many games does ◖ stand for? _____
4. Of which game were the most sold? _____ How many? _____
5. Of which game were the fewest sold? _____ How many? _____
6. Of which games were the same number sold? _____
7. How many Down the Tubes games were sold? _____
8. About how many Tanks Ahoy! games were sold? _____
9. Were more Barium Brothers or Giant Hamsters games sold? _____
10. Were fewer Bright Knights or Space Trek games sold? _____
11. About how many more El Kid games were sold than Giant Hamsters games? _____
12. About how many games were sold in all? _____

Problem Solving: Using a Pictograph

Add the ones. 15 ones equal 1 ten and 5 ones. Then add the tens.

```
 T|O
 1
 3|9
+1|6
 5|5
```

Add the ones. Then add the tens. 13 tens equal 1 hundred and 3 tens.

```
 H|T|O
   1
   |8|6
 + |5|3
 1|3|9
```

Add.

1. 19
  +32

2. 63
  +27

3. 42
  + 8

4. 36
  +36

5. 94
  +13

6. 48
  +25

7. 24
  +16

8. 58
  +61

9. 17
  +27

10. 12
   +68

11. 76
   +15

12. 41
   +92

13. 65
   +25

14. 20
   +98

15. 69
   +28

16. 29
    18
   +20

17. 31
    54
   +94

18. 44
    12
   +73

19. 22
     9
   +49

20. 80
    73
   +92

Use the scorecard to find how many points in all were scored—

	Game 1	Game 2
Jon	47	49
Ana	46	63
Tam	54	63

21. by Jon

22. by Ana

23. in game 1

24. in game 2

Adding Two-Digit Numbers

The sum of 9 tens plus 4 tens is 13 tens. 13 tens equal 1 hundred and 3 tens.

```
  H T O              H T O
  1                  1 1
  1 9 4              2 5 9
+ 1 4 5            + 5 7 3
-------            -------
  3 3 9              8 3 2
```

Sometimes you must regroup twice.

Add.

1. 735
   +158

2. 582
   +374

3. 169
   +237

4. 280
   +451

5.   93
   +509

6. 364
   +350

7. 426
   +389

8. 619
   + 14

9. 174
   +168

10. 348
   +357

11. $1.76
   +3.04

12. $2.91
   +4.53

13. $1.89
   +1.19

14. $7.45
   +0.95

15. $9.01
   +0.59

16. 348
    215
   + 57

17. 64
    907
   + 27

18. 384
    185
   +180

19. 575
     54
   + 39

20. 93
    192
   +242

Use the ad to find the cost of the following.

21. bird food and a cat brush

22. a cat brush and a dog dish

23. a dog dish and bird food

POLLY'S PETS

SALE!!

BIRD FOOD	$3.48
DOG DISH	$2.29
CAT BRUSH	$3.75

Adding Three-Digit Numbers

Regroup as many times as you need to.

Th	H	T	O		Th	H	T	O		Th	H	T	O		Th	H	T	O
	1						1				1	1				1	1	1
	2	8	6	4		4	6	0	9		1	5	4	0		3	4	8	7
+	1	7	1	0	+		6	2	6	+| 7	4	6	4	+		9	3	5
	4	5	7	4		5	2	3	5		9	0	0	4		4	4	2	2

Add.

1. 2,652
   + 826

2. 4,067
   + 380

3. 1,591
   +6,794

4. 2,671
   +4,389

5.   428
   +3,065

6. 1,496
   +2,124

7. 5,567
   +3,749

8. 6,914
   +1,303

9. 3,471
   +2,719

10. 1,940
    +2,085

11. $19.00
    + 4.25

12. $71.66
    +19.08

13. $43.88
    + 8.51

14. $14.62
    +36.49

15. $20.34
    +53.87

16. 5,481
    + 779

17.   460
    +3,150

18. 1,804
    +4,868

19. 1,974
    +2,494

20. 2,634
    +3,768

21. 4,901
    +2,948

22. 4,300
    2,726
    + 103

23. 2,649
    2,407
    +3,219

24. 1,954
    4,787
    +2,632

20

Adding Four-Digit Numbers

Sometimes a problem contains more information than you need to solve it.

At Avia Airport, 27 planes take off ~~and 32 planes land~~ before noon. After noon, 45 planes take off. How many planes take off in a day?

You don't need to know how many planes land to solve this problem. Cross out that information. Add the number of planes that take off.

```
  27
 +45
  72 planes
```

Read and think about each problem. Cross out information you do not need. Then solve the problem and check the answer.

1. A plane with 128 passengers lands. Most of them get off, but 29 stay on. Then 76 more passengers get on. How many passengers are on the plane now?

2. In boarding area A, there are 270 seats. There are 342 seats in boarding area B. There are 112 tables in both areas. How many seats are in both areas?

3. Wendy had $32.50. At the airport, she bought a book for $5.95 and a magazine for $2.75. How much did she spend?

4. Today, 3,752 suitcases came through the baggage claim. Yesterday, 4,058 came through. Of them, 37 were not claimed. How many came through in two days?

5. A plane is flying at a speed of 625 miles per hour. It has flown 475 miles so far. It has another 682 miles to go to Avia Airport. How many miles is the trip?

6. A flight from Avia to Bayo costs $192. From Bayo to Cisco, it costs $261. An airport taxi costs $18.75. How much does it cost to go from Avia to Bayo to Cisco?

7. There are 220 passengers on a plane. On their flight, 114 chicken dinners and 106 beef dinners are served. How many dinners are served?

8. Vince is reading a book during a 1,024-mile long flight. So far, he has read 166 pages. He has another 254 pages to read. How long is the book?

Problem Solving: Identifying Extra Information

You can't subtract 9 from 7.
So regroup 1 ten as 10 ones.
Now you have 5 tens and
17 ones. Subtract.

```
 T| O
 5|17
 6|7
-2|9
 3|8
```

You can't subtract 3 from 0.
Regroup 1 ten as 10 ones.
Now you have 3 tens and
10 ones. Subtract.

```
 T| O
 3|10
 4|0
-1|3
 2|7
```

Subtract.

1. 42
   −15

2. 76
   −38

3. 30
   −13

4. 88
   −29

5. 60
   − 9

6. 91
   −87

7. 57
   −28

8. 24
   − 8

9. 63
   −16

10. 96
   −39

11. 35
   −28

12. 70
   −55

13. 82
   −63

14. 53
   − 4

15. 62
   −18

16. 90
   −21

17. 24
   − 7

18. 40
   −29

19. 72
   −38

20. 83
   −46

Use the road sign to answer the following questions.

SUN VALLEY   8 km
CLEARBROOK   52 km
FARMDALE   81 km

21. How much farther is it to Clearbrook than to Sun Valley?

22. A truck driver stopped for lunch 46 kilometers after passing the sign. How much farther did she have to drive to Farmdale?

Subtracting Two-Digit Numbers

Regroup 1 hundred as 10 tens.
Now you have 11 tens.
Subtract.

```
  H|T|O
   7|11
   8|1|9
  -1|3|2
   6|8|7
```

Sometimes you must regroup more than once.

```
  H|T|O
     |14
   2|A|14
   3|5|4
  -  |8|6
   2|6|8
```

Subtract.

1. 834 − 216
2. 481 − 103
3. 951 − 422
4. 527 − 173
5. 372 − 89

6. 210 − 70
7. 623 − 478
8. 538 − 146
9. 725 − 575
10. 869 − 278

11. 240 − 27
12. 936 − 876
13. 881 − 495
14. 638 − 393
15. 971 − 182

16. $1.51 − 0.70
17. $6.70 − 1.95
18. $8.29 − 5.85
19. $5.45 − 2.49
20. $9.86 − 3.58

Use the ad to answer these questions.

 JOSH'S DELI

	POUND
SLICED HAM	$5.89
SWISS CHEESE	$4.25
AMERICAN CHEESE	$3.79

21. How much less does American cheese cost than Swiss cheese?

22. Rosalie had $7.37. She bought a pound of ham. How much money does she have left?

Subtracting Three-Digit Numbers

You can't subtract from 0. Take 1 from the next place on the left and regroup it for the 0.

```
  H T O
    6 10
  7 0̸ 6
 -1 7 2
  5 3 4
```

```
  H T O
    9
  5 10 10
  6 0̸ 0̸
 -1 9 9
  4 0 1
```

```
  H T O
    10
  8 0̸ 12
  8̸ 1̸ 2̸
 -  8 6
  8 2 6
```

Subtract.

1. 612
   −176

2. 400
   −252

3. 108
   − 29

4. 711
   −548

5. 900
   − 89

6. 700
   −363

7. 206
   − 72

8. 500
   −435

9. 413
   −124

10. 300
    −251

11. 200
    − 27

12. 504
    −111

13. 406
    −299

14. 600
    −465

15. 805
    −538

16. $1.00
    −0.59

17. $5.17
    −1.98

18. $8.00
    −3.12

19. $3.05
    −2.47

20. $9.14
    −4.58

21. Mr. Francia bought a road map for $2.79. How much change did he get from $5.00?

22. Mr. Francia is going to visit his sister in a town 307 miles away. He has driven 139 miles so far. How much farther does he have to drive?

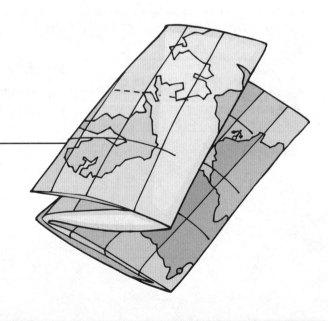

Subtracting Across Zeros

Regroup as many times as you need to.

	Th	H	T	O
	2	10		
	3̸	0̸	3	5
–	1	2	1	0
	1	8	2	5

	Th	H	T	O
		9		
	8	10	11	
	9̸	0̸	1̸	7
–		7	2	5
	8	2	9	2

	Th	H	T	O
	7	12	6	16
	8̸	2̸	7̸	6̸
–	3	9	0	8
	4	3	6	8

	Th	H	T	O
		9	9	
	6	10	10	10
	7̸	0̸	0̸	0̸
–	2	5	6	8
	4	4	3	2

Subtract.

1. 4,190
   −2,630

2. 9,685
   −1,794

3. 5,090
   −3,046

4. 8,231
   −5,357

5. 2,504
   − 495

6. 7,532
   −2,116

7. 6,308
   −4,360

8. 1,253
   − 997

9. 5,000
   −1,827

10. 9,007
    −3,882

11. 4,081
    −1,200

12. 3,652
    − 870

13. 4,736
    − 909

14. 8,615
    −4,227

15. 9,564
    −8,427

16. 4,002
    − 586

17. 9,450
    −1,196

18. 4,707
    − 423

19. 5,023
    −3,758

20. 3,841
    −1,642

21. $20.45
    − 7.19

22. $78.00
    −59.99

23. $81.72
    −12.65

24. $12.50
    − 7.86

Subtracting Four-Digit Numbers

Sometimes a problem does not contain enough information to solve it.

Eugene caught a large pike and some smaller perch while ice fishing. The pike was 32 inches long. How much longer was it than the biggest perch?

You need to know how long the biggest perch was to solve this problem. Suppose the perch was 14 inches long.

```
  32
 -14
  18 inches
```

Read and think about each problem. Write what kind of information is needed to solve it. Then make up a number and solve the problem.

1. Coldwater Lake is 22 miles long. Elizabeth is skating the length of the frozen lake. How much farther does she have to go?

2. A pair of cross-country skis regularly costs $89.95. How much will Yakov save if he buys the skis on sale?

3. A tip-up is used for ice fishing. It costs $5.25 at Doolittle's Tackle Shop. How much change will Maxine get if she buys one tip-up?

4. An ice-fishing contest was held on Coldwater Lake. There were 142 people who caught fish. How many people did not catch fish?

5. In summer, 1,007 people live in the town of Coldwater. Some of them move to Florida in winter. How many people live in Coldwater in winter?

6. First prize in the ice-fishing contest was $150.00. How much more was that than second prize?

7. The people in Coldwater own 412 snowmobiles. How many more snowmobiles do they own than cars?

8. A total of 87 inches of snow fell in Coldwater last winter. How much less is that than this winter's snowfall?

Problem Solving: Identifying Insufficient Information

Estimate sums and differences by rounding the numbers.

$$\begin{array}{r}49\\+32\end{array}$$ 50 plus 30 is 80.
The sum is about 80.

$$\begin{array}{r}\$4.06\\-2.96\end{array}$$ $4.00 minus $3.00 is $1.00.
The difference is about $1.00.

Estimate each answer. Then solve the problem and compare answers.

1. $$\begin{array}{r}\$0.21\\+0.68\\\hline \$0.89\end{array}$$ about $0.90

2. $$\begin{array}{r}59\\-15\end{array}$$ about _____

3. $$\begin{array}{r}\$0.73\\-0.54\end{array}$$ about _____

4. $$\begin{array}{r}51\\-29\end{array}$$ about _____

5. $$\begin{array}{r}\$0.87\\+0.34\end{array}$$ about _____

6. $$\begin{array}{r}24\\+45\end{array}$$ about _____

7. $$\begin{array}{r}\$8.98\\-3.09\end{array}$$ about _____

8. $$\begin{array}{r}450\\+145\end{array}$$ about _____

9. $$\begin{array}{r}\$6.22\\-4.09\end{array}$$ about _____

10. $$\begin{array}{r}\$1.95\\+7.10\end{array}$$ about _____

11. $$\begin{array}{r}997\\-506\end{array}$$ about _____

12. $$\begin{array}{r}\$2.40\\+6.72\end{array}$$ about _____

13. Dale bought paper for $1.29 and a notebook for $2.85. How much did he spend?

14. Rhonda had $5.05. She spent $2.87 for lunch. How much does she have now?

15. Melvin earned $4.60 today and $6.39 yesterday. How much has he earned in all?

Estimating Sums and Differences

Add down. Then check your answer by adding up.

1. 32   32   2.   7   7   3. 26   26   4. 51   51
    14   14↑   65   65   28   28   49   49
   +29↓ +29↑   +35   +35   +24   +24   +34   +34

5. $3.72 $3.72   6. 1,034   1,034   7. 4,108   4,108
     5.05   5.05   2,974   2,974   3,723   3,723
    +1.48   +1.48   + 584   + 584   +3,965   +3,965

Subtract. Check your answer by adding.

8.   62   19   9. 50   34   10. 95   27   11. 88   49
    -19   +43   -34   +   -27   +   -49   +
     43

12. $7.21 $4.85   13. 4,261   3,514   14. 9,806   2,998
    -4.85   +   -3,514   +   -2,998   +

Use the ad below to find the answer to each question. Check your work.

Buck's Hobbies

| SUPER Z CAR | $6.91 |
| MYSTERY RACER | $8.15 |

RACE TRACK	
STRAIGHT	$2.87
CURVED	$3.46

15. Ali got $10.00 for his birthday. How much change will he get if he buys a Mystery Racer?

16. How much less does a Super Z car cost than a Mystery Racer?

17. Gregory wants to buy a Super Z car, a Mystery Racer, and a piece of curved track. How much money does he need?

Checking Addition and Subtraction

Solve each problem. Then find each answer in the code box. Write the correct letter in each blank to solve the riddle.

1. 2,786
    +4,367

2. 6,571
    −1,679

3. 5,943
    −2,978

4. 7,015
    +5,289

5. 36,431
    −13,545

6. 27,459
    +28,568

7. 97,302
    −36,695

8. 21,872
    +45,609

9. 43,004
    −10,081

10. 15,681
    24,893
    + 9,654

11. 52,075
    −47,622

12. 67,583
    92,104
    +24,637

13. 19,267
    203,840
    +610,835

14. 743,961
    −215,237

15. 109,467
    347,006
    +201,289

── CODE ──

2,965 = T   12,304 = C   32,923 = E   528,724 = R
7,153 = S   67,481 = O   60,607 = D   657,762 = I
4,892 = H   22,886 = W   50,228 = A   833,942 = N
4,453 = L   56,027 = P   184,324 = U

Did you hear about the robbery at the laundromat?

__ __ __   __ __ __ __ __ __ __ __ __ __
3 5 8   4 11 8 3 2 9 1 6 15 13 1

__ __ __ __   __ __   __ __   __ __ __ __ __
2 9 11 7   12 6   10   1 2 15 14 3

Adding and Subtracting Large Numbers

Complete the table by using the facts that are there.

President	Born	Died	Age at Death
1. George Washington	1732	1799	_____
2. Thomas Jefferson	1743	_____	83
3. James Monroe	1758	1831	_____
4. Abraham Lincoln	_____	1865	56
5. Woodrow Wilson	1856	_____	68
6. Franklin D. Roosevelt	_____	1945	63
7. Dwight D. Eisenhower	1890	1969	_____
8. John F. Kennedy	1917	_____	46

Solve the problems below using the table you completed above.

9. George Washington was elected president in 1789. How old was he that year?

10. Thomas Jefferson wrote the Declaration of Independence. He was 33 years old when it was signed. What year was that?

11. Abraham Lincoln was 52 years old when the Civil War began. What year was that?

12. John F. Kennedy was 44 years old when he started the space program. What year was that?

Problem Solving: Finding Missing Information

Multiplying is the same as adding groups of the same size.

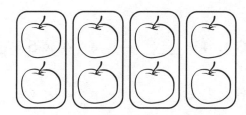

4 sets of 2 = 8
2 + 2 + 2 + 2 = 8
4 × 2 = 8

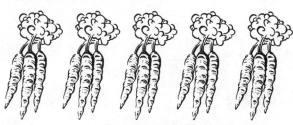

5 sets of 3 = 15
3 + 3 + 3 + 3 + 3 = 15
5 × 3 = 15

Multiply.

1. 1 × 2 = 2
2. 3 × 3 = 9
3. 2 × 2 = 4
4. 1 × 3 = 3
5. 2 × 3 = 6
6. 5 × 2 = 10
7. 6 × 3 = ___
8. 4 × 2 = 8
9. 4 × 3 = 12
10. 7 × 2 = 14
11. 9 × 3 = ___
12. 8 × 2 = 16
13. 7 × 3 = ___
14. 9 × 2 = 18
15. 8 × 3 = ___
16. 6 × 2 = 12

17. 2 × 8 = 16
18. 3 × 5 = 15
19. 2 × 1 = 2
20. 3 × 9 = ___
21. 2 × 7 = 14
22. 3 × 3 = 9

23. 3 × 6 = ___
24. 2 × 3 = 6
25. 3 × 4 = ___
26. 2 × 9 = 18
27. 3 × 8 = ___
28. 2 × 4 = 8

29. 2 × 2 = 4
30. 3 × 7 = ___
31. 2 × 5 = 10
32. 3 × 2 = 6
33. 2 × 8 = 18
34. 3 × 1 = 3

35. Pamela bought 5 packs of tomatoes. There were 3 tomatoes in each pack. How many tomatoes did Pamela buy?

36. Natalie bought 6 packs of peppers. There are 2 peppers in each pack. How many peppers did Natalie buy?

Multiplying 2s and 3s

Multiply.

1. 1 × 4 = 4
2. 2 × 5 = 10
3. 3 × 4 = ___
4. 4 × 5 = ___
5. 3 × 5 = ___
6. 2 × 4 = 8
7. 6 × 5 = ___
8. 4 × 4 = 16
9. 1 × 5 = 5
10. 5 × 4 = ___
11. 8 × 5 = ___
12. 6 × 4 = ___
13. 9 × 4 = ___
14. 7 × 5 = ___
15. 7 × 4 = ___
16. 9 × 5 = ___

17. 4 × 8 = ___
18. 5 × 6 = ___
19. 4 × 4 = 16
20. 5 × 8 = ___
21. 4 × 1 = 4
22. 5 × 2 = 10

23. 5 × 7 = ___
24. 4 × 5 = ___
25. 5 × 3 = 15
26. 4 × 9 = ___
27. 5 × 5 = 25
28. 4 × 6 = ___

29. 4 × 2 = 8
30. 5 × 9 = ___
31. 4 × 3 = 12
32. 5 × 1 = 5
33. 4 × 7 = ___
34. 5 × 4 = ___

35. Seth set up 6 tables for his party. He will have 4 people sit at each table. How many people will be at the party?

36. Naoki bought 9 bags of balloons. In each bag, there are 5 balloons. How many balloons did she buy?

37. Seth bought 8 bags of pretzels. Each bag contains 4 servings. How many servings did Seth get?

38. Naoki bought 7 packs of invitations. There are 5 in each pack. How many invitations did she buy?

Multiplying 4s and 5s

The product remains the same when the order of the factors changes.

 $\begin{array}{r}2\\\times 3\\\hline 6\end{array}$ Factors $\begin{array}{r}3\\\times 2\\\hline 6\end{array}$
Product

Multiply.

1. $\begin{array}{r}4\\\times 3\\\hline 12\end{array}$ 2. $\begin{array}{r}3\\\times 4\\\hline 12\end{array}$ 3. $\begin{array}{r}5\\\times 2\\\hline 10\end{array}$ 4. $\begin{array}{r}2\\\times 5\\\hline 10\end{array}$ 5. $\begin{array}{r}2\\\times 4\\\hline 8\end{array}$ 6. $\begin{array}{r}4\\\times 2\\\hline 8\end{array}$

When 1 is a factor, the product is the other factor.

 $\begin{array}{r}1\\\times 6\\\hline 6\end{array}$ $\begin{array}{r}6\\\times 1\\\hline 6\end{array}$

Multiply.

7. $\begin{array}{r}1\\\times 4\\\hline 4\end{array}$ 8. $\begin{array}{r}5\\\times 1\\\hline 5\end{array}$ 9. $\begin{array}{r}3\\\times 1\\\hline 3\end{array}$ 10. $\begin{array}{r}1\\\times 2\\\hline 2\end{array}$ 11. $\begin{array}{r}1\\\times 1\\\hline 1\end{array}$ 12. $\begin{array}{r}8\\\times 1\\\hline 8\end{array}$

When 0 is a factor, the product is 0.

   $\begin{array}{r}0\\\times 4\\\hline 0\end{array}$ $\begin{array}{r}4\\\times 0\\\hline 0\end{array}$

Multiply.

13. $\begin{array}{r}3\\\times 0\\\hline 3\end{array}$ 14. $\begin{array}{r}0\\\times 5\\\hline 5\end{array}$ 15. $\begin{array}{r}1\\\times 0\\\hline 1\end{array}$ 16. $\begin{array}{r}2\\\times 0\\\hline 2\end{array}$ 17. $\begin{array}{r}0\\\times 6\\\hline 6\end{array}$ 18. $\begin{array}{r}0\\\times 9\\\hline 9\end{array}$

Properties of Multiplication

Multiply.

1. $1 \times 6 =$ _____
2. $3 \times 7 =$ _____
3. $5 \times 6 =$ _____
4. $1 \times 7 =$ _____
5. $2 \times 7 =$ _____
6. $7 \times 6 =$ _____
7. $4 \times 7 =$ _____
8. $6 \times 6 =$ _____
9. $3 \times 6 =$ _____
10. $6 \times 7 =$ _____
11. $9 \times 6 =$ _____
12. $7 \times 7 =$ _____
13. $8 \times 7 =$ _____
14. $4 \times 6 =$ _____
15. $5 \times 7 =$ _____
16. $8 \times 6 =$ _____

17. $\begin{array}{r} 6 \\ \times 2 \\ \hline \end{array}$
18. $\begin{array}{r} 7 \\ \times 9 \\ \hline \end{array}$
19. $\begin{array}{r} 6 \\ \times 6 \\ \hline \end{array}$
20. $\begin{array}{r} 7 \\ \times 7 \\ \hline \end{array}$
21. $\begin{array}{r} 6 \\ \times 9 \\ \hline \end{array}$
22. $\begin{array}{r} 7 \\ \times 3 \\ \hline \end{array}$

23. $\begin{array}{r} 7 \\ \times 1 \\ \hline \end{array}$
24. $\begin{array}{r} 6 \\ \times 3 \\ \hline \end{array}$
25. $\begin{array}{r} 7 \\ \times 4 \\ \hline \end{array}$
26. $\begin{array}{r} 6 \\ \times 7 \\ \hline \end{array}$
27. $\begin{array}{r} 7 \\ \times 8 \\ \hline \end{array}$
28. $\begin{array}{r} 6 \\ \times 5 \\ \hline \end{array}$

29. $\begin{array}{r} 6 \\ \times 4 \\ \hline \end{array}$
30. $\begin{array}{r} 7 \\ \times 6 \\ \hline \end{array}$
31. $\begin{array}{r} 6 \\ \times 8 \\ \hline \end{array}$
32. $\begin{array}{r} 7 \\ \times 9 \\ \hline \end{array}$
33. $\begin{array}{r} 6 \\ \times 2 \\ \hline \end{array}$
34. $\begin{array}{r} 7 \\ \times 5 \\ \hline \end{array}$

35. Isaak added 7 pages to his album. He put 6 photographs on each page. How many photos did he add to his album?

36. Miya went on vacation for 8 days. She took 7 pictures each day. How many pictures did she take on her vacation?

37. There are 7 shelves at Mr. Gianni's camera shop. On each one, 7 cameras are displayed. How many cameras are displayed in all?

38. Theresa stores her pictures in 9 boxes. There are 6 packs of pictures in each box. How many packs of pictures are there?

Multiplying 6s and 7s

Multiply.

1. 2 × 8 = ___
2. 1 × 9 = ___
3. 4 × 8 = ___
4. 2 × 9 = ___

5. 3 × 9 = ___
6. 5 × 8 = ___
7. 4 × 9 = ___
8. 1 × 8 = ___

9. 6 × 8 = ___
10. 7 × 9 = ___
11. 8 × 8 = ___
12. 9 × 9 = ___

13. 5 × 9 = ___
14. 7 × 8 = ___
15. 8 × 9 = ___
16. 9 × 8 = ___

17. 9
    ×6

18. 8
    ×3

19. 9
    ×9

20. 8
    ×5

21. 9
    ×2

22. 8
    ×8

23. 8
    ×6

24. 9
    ×7

25. 8
    ×2

26. 9
    ×6

27. 8
    ×7

28. 9
    ×3

29. 9
    ×1

30. 8
    ×4

31. 9
    ×5

32. 8
    ×9

33. 9
    ×4

34. 8
    ×1

35. Claudia has 9 packs of bubble gum. Each pack holds 8 pieces. How many pieces of bubble gum does Claudia have?

36. A giant-size bar of chocolate is marked off into little blocks. There are 8 rows of 8 blocks. How many blocks are there?

37. Luigi has 7 rolls of mints. There are 9 mints in each roll. How many mints does he have?

38. There are 9 bags of gummi worms on display. If there are 9 worms in each bag, how many worms are on display?

Multiplying 8s and 9s

35

You can write a number sentence to solve a problem.

Mrs. Harris grilled 2 packs of hamburgers. There were 8 hamburgers in each pack. How many hamburgers did she grill?

$2 \times 8 = 16$ hamburgers

Write a number sentence to solve each problem.

1. A pound of ground beef makes 5 hamburgers. How many hamburgers can Kirsten make from 9 pounds of beef?

2. Duane put 8 hamburgers on the grill. He topped 4 of them with cheese. How many were plain?

3. There are 3 bowls of potato salad. Each bowl holds 8 servings. How many servings are there altogether?

4. Mr. Harris bought 6 packs of hamburger buns. If each pack holds 8 buns, how many buns did he buy?

5. A can of frozen drink mix makes 9 servings. How many servings will Russell make if he mixes 6 cans?

6. A pie was cut into 9 slices. A cake was cut into 8 pieces. How many pieces of dessert were there?

7. A box holds 9 doughnuts. How many doughnuts are in 9 boxes?

8. A can of baked beans contains 4 servings. Sarah opened 8 cans. How many servings did she prepare?

Problem Solving: Writing a Number Sentence

1 × 3 = 3   1 × 4 = 4
2 × 3 = 6   2 × 4 = 8   The products 3, 6, 9, 12, and 15 are **multiples** of 3.
3 × 3 = 9   3 × 4 = 12   The products 4, 8, 12, 16, and 20 are multiples of 4.
4 × 3 = 12 4 × 4 = 16   The product 12 is a **common multiple** of 3 and 4.
5 × 3 = 15 5 × 4 = 20

Find the missing multiples.

1. 2: 2, 4, ____, ____, ____, ____, ____, ____, ____, ____, ____, ____

2. 3: 3, 6, ____, 12, ____, 18, ____, ____, ____, ____, 33, ____, 39

3. 4: 4, ____, ____, ____, 20, ____, ____, ____, 36, ____, ____, 48

4. 5: 5, ____, ____, ____, ____, ____, ____, 40, ____, ____, 55, 60

5. 6: 6, 12, ____, ____, ____, 36, ____, ____, ____, 60, ____, 72

6. 7: 7, ____, ____, ____, ____, 42, ____, ____, 63, ____

7. 8: 8, ____, ____, ____, 40, ____, ____, ____, 72, 80

8. 9: ____, 18, ____, 36, ____, ____, ____, ____, 81, ____

Use your work above to find at least two common multiples of each pair of numbers.

9. 2, 3 _____

10. 3, 4 _____

11. 2, 5 _____

12. 3, 5 _____

13. 3, 6 _____

14. 4, 5 _____

15. 4, 6 _____

16. 6, 8 _____

17. 3, 9 _____

18. 2, 8 _____

Finding Multiples

Complete the multiplication table.

×	0	1	2	3	4	5	6	7	8	9
0										
1										
2										
3										
4										
5										
6										
7										
8										
9										

Fill in each box with the missing factor or product. Use the table above to help you.

1. $3 \times \square = 12$
2. $8 \times \square = 8$
3. $\square \times 9 = 0$
4. $9 \times 3 = \square$

5. $\square \times 4 = 24$
6. $7 \times 2 = \square$
7. $6 \times \square = 48$
8. $\square \times 9 = 63$

9. $4 \times 8 = \square$
10. $\square \times 8 = 56$
11. $\square \times 7 = 28$
12. $5 \times \square = 40$

13. $\square \times 6 = 54$
14. $9 \times \square = 45$
15. $4 \times 9 = \square$
16. $\square \times 9 = 81$

17. $8 \times \square = 64$
18. $\square \times 9 = 72$
19. $\square \times 7 = 49$
20. $8 \times \square = 48$

Multiplication and Missing Factors

Dividing is like subtracting groups of the same size.

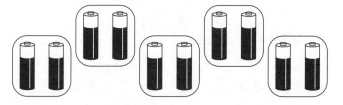
5 sets of 2 in 10
10 divided by 2 = 5
10 ÷ 2 = 5

4 sets of 3 in 12
12 divided by 3 = 4
12 ÷ 3 = 4

Divide.

1. 4 ÷ 2 = _____
2. 3 ÷ 3 = _____
3. 8 ÷ 2 = _____
4. 12 ÷ 3 = _____

5. 9 ÷ 3 = _____
6. 2 ÷ 2 = _____
7. 15 ÷ 3 = _____
8. 10 ÷ 2 = _____

9. 6 ÷ 2 = _____
10. 21 ÷ 3 = _____
11. 12 ÷ 2 = _____
12. 6 ÷ 3 = _____

13. 27 ÷ 3 = _____
14. 16 ÷ 2 = _____
15. 18 ÷ 3 = _____
16. 14 ÷ 2 = _____

17. 2)̅1̅4̅
18. 3)̅2̅4̅
19. 2)̅1̅8̅
20. 3)̅6̅
21. 2)̅1̅2̅

22. 3)̅2̅1̅
23. 2)̅1̅0̅
24. 3)̅9̅
25. 3)̅1̅5̅
26. 3)̅2̅7̅

27. 2)̅1̅6̅
28. 3)̅1̅2̅
29. 2)̅8̅
30. 3)̅1̅8̅
31. 2)̅6̅

32. There are 16 batteries on display. They come in packs of 2 batteries. How many packs are on display?

33. There are 18 CDs on the shelf. They are placed in stacks of 3 CDs. How many stacks are there?

Dividing by 2 and 3

Divide.

1. 8 ÷ 4 = _____
2. 5 ÷ 5 = _____
3. 20 ÷ 4 = _____
4. 15 ÷ 5 = _____

5. 20 ÷ 5 = _____
6. 28 ÷ 4 = _____
7. 10 ÷ 5 = _____
8. 4 ÷ 4 = _____

9. 16 ÷ 4 = _____
10. 25 ÷ 5 = _____
11. 12 ÷ 4 = _____
12. 35 ÷ 5 = _____

13. 30 ÷ 5 = _____
14. 24 ÷ 4 = _____
15. 40 ÷ 5 = _____
16. 36 ÷ 4 = _____

17. 4)32
18. 5)5
19. 4)20
20. 5)45
21. 4)24

22. 5)30
23. 4)28
24. 5)40
25. 4)12
26. 5)15

27. 4)36
28. 5)10
29. 4)4
30. 5)35
31. 4)16

32. Zachary wants to buy 24 lightbulbs. They come in packs of 4. How many packs should he buy?

33. Yolanda needs 35 bolts. If there are 5 bolts in a pack, how many packs should she get?

34. Brandon bought a bag of 12 floor protectors. If he puts 4 on the legs of each chair, how many chairs can he do?

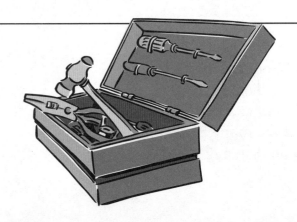

Dividing by 4 and 5

Use multiplication facts to help you divide and to check your division.

$$24 \div 4 = 6 \text{ because } 6 \times 4 = 24$$

Quotient ↑ ↑ ↑ ↑
Dividend Divisor Factor

Divide. Think of multiplication.

1. $20 \div 5 =$ _____
   $\square \times 5 = 20$

2. $32 \div 4 =$ _____
   $\square \times 4 = 32$

3. $15 \div 3 =$ _____
   $\square \times 3 = 15$

4. $18 \div 2 =$ _____
   $\square \times 2 = 18$

5. $27 \div 3 =$ _____
   $\square \times 3 = 27$

6. $16 \div 4 =$ _____
   $\square \times 4 = 16$

7. $28 \div 4 =$ _____
   $\square \times 4 = 28$

8. $40 \div 5 =$ _____
   $\square \times 5 = 40$

9. $24 \div 3 =$ _____
   $\square \times 3 = 24$

Divide. Check by multiplying.

10. $2\overline{)14}$ (×←7, 14; ×7, 14)

11. $1\overline{)5}$

12. $4\overline{)20}$

13. $3\overline{)3}$

14. $4\overline{)4}$

15. $2\overline{)12}$

16. $5\overline{)30}$

17. $4\overline{)36}$

18. $4\overline{)12}$

19. $5\overline{)25}$

20. $3\overline{)18}$

21. $5\overline{)35}$

22. $3\overline{)21}$

23. $2\overline{)16}$

24. $5\overline{)45}$

25. $3\overline{)12}$

Division, the Inverse of Multiplication

Divide.

1. 14 ÷ 7 = _____
2. 6 ÷ 6 = _____
3. 21 ÷ 7 = _____
4. 12 ÷ 6 = _____

5. 18 ÷ 6 = _____
6. 28 ÷ 7 = _____
7. 42 ÷ 6 = _____
8. 7 ÷ 7 = _____

9. 35 ÷ 7 = _____
10. 54 ÷ 6 = _____
11. 49 ÷ 7 = _____
12. 24 ÷ 6 = _____

13. 48 ÷ 6 = _____
14. 63 ÷ 7 = _____
15. 30 ÷ 6 = _____
16. 56 ÷ 7 = _____

17. 7)42
18. 6)36
19. 7)14
20. 6)48
21. 7)28

22. 6)18
23. 7)56
24. 6)54
25. 7)42
26. 6)30

27. 7)49
28. 6)42
29. 7)63
30. 6)24
31. 7)21

32. A total of 48 people signed up for pottery classes. If one box of clay is enough for 6 people, how many boxes are needed?

_____

33. Charlene decorated a clay dish with 49 stars. She put the stars in rows of 7 stars. How many rows of stars are on the dish?

_____

34. Mr. Ishihara wants to display his students' pots. He has 63 pots and can put 7 pots on a shelf. How many shelves will he need?

Dividing by 6 and 7

Divide.

1. $9 \div 9 =$ _____
2. $16 \div 8 =$ _____
3. $27 \div 9 =$ _____
4. $8 \div 8 =$ _____

5. $24 \div 8 =$ _____
6. $18 \div 9 =$ _____
7. $48 \div 8 =$ _____
8. $45 \div 9 =$ _____

9. $81 \div 9 =$ _____
10. $56 \div 8 =$ _____
11. $72 \div 9 =$ _____
12. $64 \div 8 =$ _____

13. $40 \div 8 =$ _____
14. $63 \div 9 =$ _____
15. $32 \div 8 =$ _____
16. $54 \div 9 =$ _____

17. $9\overline{)36}$
18. $8\overline{)72}$
19. $9\overline{)18}$
20. $8\overline{)32}$
21. $9\overline{)63}$

22. $8\overline{)48}$
23. $9\overline{)81}$
24. $8\overline{)56}$
25. $9\overline{)72}$
26. $8\overline{)16}$

27. $9\overline{)27}$
28. $8\overline{)64}$
29. $9\overline{)54}$
30. $8\overline{)24}$
31. $9\overline{)45}$

32. Jasmin has 64 special pennies in her coin collection. She puts 8 pennies in a row. How many rows will she make?

33. Ivan has 45 coins from foreign countries. If he has 9 coins from each country, how many countries are represented?

34. The coin club has 72 members. At a dinner meeting, 8 people sit at each table. How many tables are there?

Dividing by 8 and 9

Sometimes a problem has two steps.

Allison had $6.00 for lunch. She bought a hamburger for $2.95 and french fries for $1.30. How much money did she have left?

First, add.
$2.95
+1.30
$4.25

Then subtract.
$6.00
−4.25
$1.75

Read each problem. Think about the two steps needed to solve it. Then solve the problem and check the answer.

1. There are 173 people in line for a ride. The ride has 8 cars that hold 6 people each. If no more people get in line, how many will be waiting after the next ride fills up?

2. Hans bought a T-shirt for $14.50 and a hat for $7.96. How much money did he have left from $30.00?

3. A one-day pass to the park costs $54.88. After six o'clock, a pass costs $35.95. Parking always costs $4.50. How much can Audrey save if she walks to the park and goes after six o'clock?

4. A show at the park lasts 48 minutes. For the first 18 minutes, performers tell jokes. For the rest of the time, they sing 6 songs. If the songs are of equal length, what is the longest a song could be?

5. Lee works 35 hours a week at the park. He works the same number of hours on each of 5 days. He earns $8 an hour. How much does he earn in one day?

Problem Solving: Planning Two-Step Solutions

12 = 1 × 12   18 = 1 × 18   1, 2, 3, 4, 6, and 12 are **factors** of 12.
12 = 2 × 6   18 = 2 × 9   1, 2, 3, 6, 9, and 18 are factors of 18.
12 = 3 × 4   18 = 3 × 6   1, 2, 3, and 6 are **common factors** of 12 and 18.

Find the missing factors.

1. 6: 1, 2, ___, 6
2. 8: 1, 2, ___, 8
3. 9: 1, ___, 9
4. 10: 1, ___, ___, 10
5. 15: 1, ___, ___, 15
6. 20: 1, 2, ___, ___, 10, 20
7. 24: 1, 2, ___, 4, ___, 8, 12, 24
8. 25: 1, ___, 25

9. 27: 1, ___, ___, 27
10. 28: 1, 2, ___, ___, 14, 28
11. 30: 1, 2, 3, ___, ___, 10, 15, 30
12. 35: 1, ___, ___, 35
13. 36: 1, 2, 3, 4, ___, 9, 12, 18, 36
14. 40: 1, 2, 4, ___, ___, 10, 20, 40
15. 45: 1, 3, ___, ___, 15, 45
16. 48: 1, 2, 3, 4, ___, 8, 12, 16, 24, 48

Use your work above to find the common factors of each pair of numbers.

17. 6, 8 _____
18. 8, 12 _____
19. 6, 12 _____
20. 9, 15 _____
21. 12, 20 _____

22. 12, 30 _____
23. 18, 27 _____
24. 24, 36 _____
25. 28, 35 _____
26. 36, 48 _____

Finding Factors   45

13 lightbulbs

4 groups of 3 lightbulbs

1 lightbulb left over

Divide. Write the remainder after the quotient. Check by multiplying, and then adding the remainder to the product.

1. 2)9̄   4 R1   ×4   2
        8   8
        1   +1
                   9

2. 5)17̄   3. 8)44̄   4. 3)25̄

5. 9)26̄   6. 6)41̄   7. 5)13̄   8. 7)46̄

9. 9)82̄   10. 4)14̄   11. 7)51̄   12. 8)67̄

13. 5)49̄   14. 4)37̄   15. 8)43̄   16. 6)26̄

17. 2)15̄   18. 6)35̄   19. 3)28̄   20. 9)60̄

46   Division with Remainders

Sometimes a problem has a remainder.

Mrs. Kim had 55 plants. She planted them in rows of 7 plants. How many full rows were there? How many rows in all?

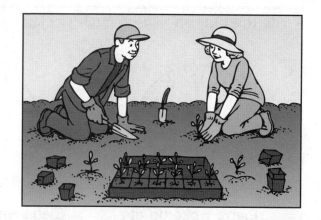

First, divide.

```
      7 R6
   7 ) 55
       49
        6
```

Now think.
There are 7 full rows and another row of 6. So Mrs. Kim made 8 rows.

Read each problem and divide. Think about the quotient and the remainder. Then answer the question.

1. Mr. Kim had 17 fruit trees. He planted them in rows of 6. How many rows did he make? How many trees were in the rows?

2. Dora planted 86 tulip bulbs in groups of 9 and put the extras in a pot. How many groups did Dora make? How many bulbs were in the pot?

3. Ken cut 43 roses. He put 6 roses in each vase and gave the rest to his neighbor. How many vases did he fill? How many roses did his neighbor get?

4. Becca needed 68 plastic flowerpots. They came in packs of 8 pots. How many packs did Becca have to buy?

5. Jason planted the same number of petunias in each of 5 window boxes. If he started with 22 petunias, how many did he put in each box? How many were left over?

6. Diana had 29 pumpkin seeds. She planted 4 seeds in each mound. How many mounds did she make? How many seeds were left?

7. Stan has 25 rosebushes to water. The watering can holds enough to water 3 bushes. How many times will Stan have to fill the can?

8. Iwa had 50 asters. She planted them in rows of 6. How many rows did she make? How many asters were left over?

Problem Solving: Interpreting a Remainder

Write the time shown on each clock.

1.
Pierre woke up at ___6:00___.

2.
Elena went to the dentist at _____.

3.
The school bus arrives at _____.

4.
Kazuo's watch stopped at _____.

5.
The movie was over at _____.

6.
Nancy got home at _____.

Complete.

7.
___ minutes before ___
___ minutes after ___

8.
___ minutes before ___
___ minutes after ___

9.
___ minutes before ___
___ minutes after ___

10.
___ minutes before ___
___ minutes after ___

11.
___ minutes before ___
___ minutes after ___

12.
___ minutes before ___
___ minutes after ___

Time: Hours and Minutes

Sometimes a problem asks you to find a time or an amount of time.

It is 7:35. The bus will be here in 15 minutes. What time will the bus be here?

In 15 minutes, it will be 7:50.

Emma catches the bus at 7:50 and gets off at 8:10. How long is the ride?

From 7:50 to 8:10 is 20 minutes. So the ride is 20 minutes long.

Find each answer.

1. Mikhail started lunch at 11:50. It was ready 20 minutes later. What time was it ready?

2. Maria's piano lesson starts at 9:00. She left the house at 8:25. How long does it take to get to her lesson?

3. Damon went to bed at 10:45. He slept for 8 hours. What time did he get up?

4. The movie started at 7:30. It was over at 9:20. How long did the movie last?

5. Margaret walked her dog from 5:15 to 6:05. How long did the walk take?

6. The baseball game was over at 2:00. If the game lasted 2 hours 30 minutes, what time had it started?

7. The Leongs left for a trip at 4:00 A.M. They arrived at their hotel at 2:30 P.M. How long did their trip take?

8. A plane was expected to land at 11:40. It arrived 1 hour 15 minutes late. What time did it arrive?

Problem Solving: Finding Elapsed Time

60 seconds = 1 minute
60 minutes = 1 hour
24 hours = 1 day
7 days = 1 week
52 weeks = 1 year
365 days = 1 year
12 months = 1 year

Use the information above to help you find the answer to each word problem.

1. Solomon ran a half mile in 1 minute 58 seconds. How many seconds is that in all?

2. Mei Lin practiced the trombone 1 hour 15 minutes yesterday but only 50 minutes today. How much more did she practice yesterday?

3. Mr. McFarland's car battery is guaranteed for 42 months. How many years and months is that?

4. The winners of the dance contest danced for 36 hours. How many days and hours is that?

5. January has 31 days. How many full weeks and days are there?

6. Mrs. Mendoza worked 245 days this year. The rest of the days were weekends, holidays, and vacations. How many days did she not work?

7. Alfonso went to school 38 weeks this year. How many weeks of vacation did he get?

8. It took 28 days for Olivia's seeds to sprout. How many weeks was that?

Problem Solving: Using Units of Time

Penny	Nickel	Dime	Quarter	Half-Dollar	Dollar Bill
1¢	5¢	10¢	25¢	50¢	100¢
$0.01	$0.05	$0.10	$0.25	$0.50	$1.00

Write the number of each coin or bill you would use to pay for each item.

Item and Price	Dollars	Half-Dollars	Quarters	Dimes	Nickels	Pennies
1. $9.89	9	1	1	1	—	4
2. $3.79						
3. $6.14						
4. $7.12						
5. $0.45						
6. $2.28						
7. $4.46						

Money

Trent bought a soda for $0.59. He paid for it with a dollar bill. How much change did he get?

Make change by counting **up** from the price to the amount given in payment. For example, for $0.59—

Give: 1¢   +   5¢   +   10¢   +   25¢
         (a penny) (a nickel) (a dime) (a quarter)

Say: "60¢"   "65¢"   "75¢"   "$1.00"

The amount of change is $0.41.

Make change for each purchase below. Use the fewest coins possible. If you do not need a kind of coin, leave that space blank.

Price	Amount Paid		Pennies	Nickels	Dimes	Quarters	Half-Dollars	Dollars	Total Change
1. kite $7.88	$10.00	Give	2¢	—	10¢	—	—	$2.00	$2.12
		Say	$7.90		$8.00			$10.00	
2. popsicle $0.45	$1.00	Give							
		Say							
3. fries $1.11	$2.00	Give							
		Say							
4. fishbowl $2.29	$5.00	Give							
		Say							
5. necklace $0.76	$1.00	Give							
		Say							
6. crayons $4.95	$10.00	Give							
		Say							

52   **Making Change**

When 10 is a factor, the product is the other factor with one 0 after it.

$$\begin{array}{r} 10 \\ \times 4 \\ \hline 40 \end{array} \qquad \begin{array}{r} 25 \\ \times 10 \\ \hline 250 \end{array}$$

Multiply.

1. 10 × 8
2. 10 × 5
3. 9 × 10
4. 51 × 10
5. 12 × 10
6. 10 × 84

When 100 is a factor, the product is the other factor with two 0s after it.

$$\begin{array}{r} 100 \\ \times 8 \\ \hline 800 \end{array} \qquad \begin{array}{r} 32 \\ \times 100 \\ \hline 3{,}200 \end{array}$$

Multiply.

7. 100 × 5
8. 2 × 100
9. 100 × 63
10. 18 × 100
11. 100 × 90
12. 100 × 26

Sometimes a factor is a multiple of 10 or 100. The product will have the same number of 0s as the factor.

$$\begin{array}{r} 2 \\ \times 6 \\ \hline 12 \end{array} \qquad \begin{array}{r} 20 \\ \times 6 \\ \hline 120 \end{array} \qquad \begin{array}{r} 200 \\ \times 6 \\ \hline 1{,}200 \end{array}$$

Multiply.

13. 40 × 2
14. 50 × 9
15. 200 × 4
16. 30 × 5
17. 600 × 3
18. 700 × 8

19. 60 × 7
20. 900 × 6
21. 30 × 9
22. 400 × 3
23. 80 × 4
24. 200 × 5

25. Ms. Nelson's car gets 35 miles to a gallon of gas. How many miles can it travel on 10 gallons of gas?

26. The printer delivered 5 boxes of 500 tickets each for the school play. How many tickets were printed?

Extending Multiplication: Multiples of 10 and 100

Multiply the ones. Then multiply the tens.

1. 23 × 3
2. 34 × 2
3. 11 × 8
4. 12 × 4
5. 13 × 3
6. 41 × 2

7. 64 × 2
8. 31 × 5
9. 43 × 3
10. 72 × 4
11. 84 × 2
12. 21 × 7

Multiply the ones and regroup as ones and tens. Then multiply the tens and add the tens from the regrouping.

```
  1          3
 24         47
× 4        × 5
 96        235
```

Multiply.

13. 14 × 6
14. 33 × 9
15. 12 × 8
16. 24 × 5
17. 69 × 3
18. 98 × 2

19. 49 × 4
20. 56 × 6
21. 64 × 7
22. 17 × 3
23. 27 × 8
24. 38 × 5

25. 93 × 4
26. 58 × 8
27. 65 × 2
28. 18 × 7
29. 36 × 9
30. 74 × 6

31. Mrs. O'Brien's hens laid 9 dozen eggs today. Since a dozen is 12, how many eggs did the hens lay?

32. Mrs. O'Brien had 27 cans of milk waiting for the milk truck. If a can holds 6 gallons, how many gallons of milk did Mrs. O'Brien have?

Multiply the ones, then the tens, and finally the hundreds.

1. 324
   ×2

2. 132
   ×3

3. 201
   ×4

4. 310
   ×6

5. 611
   ×5

Multiply and regroup. Remember to add the tens or hundreds from the regrouping.

Sometimes you must regroup twice.

```
  3         1        2 1
 219      130     1,174
  ×4       ×6       ×3
 ───      ───     ─────
 876      780     3,522
```

Multiply.

6. 349
   ×2

7. 191
   ×6

8. 473
   ×3

9. 506
   ×5

10. 731
    ×8

11. 250
    ×4

12. 261
    ×7

13. 528
    ×9

14. 806
    ×2

15. 189
    ×5

16. 4,236
    ×2

17. 1,015
    ×5

18. 1,251
    ×7

19. 2,309
    ×3

20. 1,072
    ×9

21. $3.51
    ×7

22. $4.37
    ×2

23. $2.86
    ×8

24. $5.40
    ×5

25. $9.23
    ×4

26. Mr. Paolini works 8 hours a day. He worked 249 days last year. How many hours did he work last year?

27. Mrs. Quan earns $18.05 an hour. How much does she earn in 7 hours?

Multiplying Three- and Four-Digit Numbers

Use the bar graph to answer each question and solve each problem.

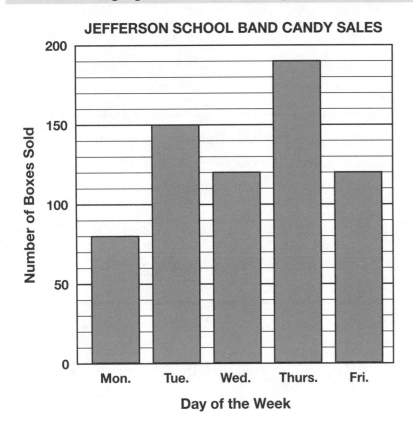

1. What does the bar graph show? _____

2. What do the numbers on the left side stand for? _____

3. How many boxes were sold on Tuesday? _____

4. On which day were the fewest boxes sold? _____

5. On which day were the most boxes sold? _____

6. On which days were the same number of boxes sold? _____

7. How many more boxes were sold on Thursday than on Monday?

8. What was the total number of boxes sold that week?

Problem Solving: Using a Bar Graph

Divide the tens or hundreds. Then multiply the quotient and the divisor. Subtract the product. Now repeat for the next place.

```
        43 ← Quotient
     2)86  ← Dividend
      -8
        6
       -6
```
Divisor

```
       144
     3)432
      -3
       13
      -12
        12
        12
```

Divide.

1. 2)284
2. 3)69
3. 4)848
4. 2)68
5. 3)693

6. 8)96
7. 7)840
8. 2)74
9. 5)905
10. 6)90

11. 4)824
12. 8)976
13. 5)825
14. 3)444
15. 2)794

16. A park ranger used a 48-pound bag of bird seed to fill feeders. If she put 4 pounds in each feeder, how many feeders did she fill?

17. The rangers unpacked 744 park maps. If the same number of maps came in each of 6 boxes, how many maps came in a box?

Dividing Two- and Three-Digit Numbers

The 1 in the hundreds place can't be divided by 6.
Regroup 1 hundred as 10 tens.
Divide the total tens: 18 ÷ 6 = 3.
Be careful to put the answer in the correct place.

```
        31
     _____
  6 ) 186
     -18
     ____
        6
       -6
```

Divide. Be careful to put the quotients in the correct places.

1. 4)216   2. 5)350   3. 2)164   4. 3)249

5. 6)426   6. 8)272   7. 9)558   8. 7)644

9. 4)$1.72   10. 7)$3.78   11. 5)$3.45   12. 8)$6.96

13. 3)1,782   14. 2)1,930   15. 7)3,332   16. 4)2,832

17. A bakery baked 384 cupcakes today. How many packages of 4 cupcakes is that?

18. Today, 6 bakery trucks were loaded with 3,870 loaves of bread. Each truck carried the same number of loaves. How many did each truck carry?

Dividing Three- and Four-Digit Numbers

To find an average, add and then divide.

Gina scored 18, 26, 18, 24, and 19 points in 5 basketball games. What was her average score?

First, add the scores. Then divide the sum by the number of games played.

The average score was 21 points.

```
 18        21
 26     5)105
 18       10
 24        5
+19        5
---
105
```

Add and divide to find each average.

1. Ian weighs 125 pounds. Rasheed weighs 135 pounds. What is their average weight?

2. Loretta ran 4 miles Monday, 3 miles Wednesday, and 8 miles Saturday. What is the average number of miles she ran?

3. Tao made 3 long-distance phone calls. They cost $1.25, $4.61, and $1.88. What was the average cost of a call?

4. Rebecca recorded the temperature 5 times today: 78°F, 83°F, 91°F, 86°F, and 77°F. What was the average?

5. Mr. Takahashi spent $6.12 on breakfast and $8.78 on lunch. What was the average cost of a meal?

6. Grace has 3 dogs. They weigh 17, 52, and 63 pounds each. What is the average weight of Grace's dogs?

7. Jorge and Valerie went on 4 hikes. The hikes were 16, 25, 31, and 12 miles long. What was the average length?

8. On 3 days, Ralph rode a roller coaster 18, 11, and 22 times. What was the average number of rides per day?

Problem Solving: Finding Averages

Estimate products and quotients by rounding the numbers to be multiplied or divided.

57 is about 60.
6 times 60 is 360.
So the answer is about 360.

$$\begin{array}{r} 57 \\ \times\,6 \\ \hline \end{array}$$

$3.15 is about $3.00.
$3.00 divided by 5 is $0.60.
So the answer is about $0.60.

5)$3.15

Estimate each answer. Then solve the problem and compare answers.

1. 78 × 8 = 624   about 640

2. 7)672   about _____

3. $0.87 × 4   about _____

4. 5)295   about _____

5. $0.49 × 9   about _____

6. 6)498   about _____

7. 4)$3.56   about _____

8. $1.95 × 3   about _____

9. 9)459   about _____

10. A large pizza costs $9.15. If 3 people share a large pizza, how much does each person's share cost?

11. A small pizza costs $6.92. Hannah sold 8 of them. How much money did she collect?

12. Mrs. Torres bought 5 party pizzas at $12.10 each. How much did she spend?

Estimating Products and Quotients

A number sentence may have more than one operation. Do the operations in this order.

1. Do the work inside parentheses first.
2. Next, multiply and divide from left to right.
3. Finally, add and subtract from left to right.

Follow the order of operations to solve each problem.

1. $2 \times 8 + 6 =$

2. $3 \times (13 - 6) =$

3. $48 - 18 \div 3 =$

4. $(8 + 16) \div 8 =$

5. $64 \div 8 - 2 =$

6. $72 - 36 \div 6 =$

7. $(3 + 6) \times 9 =$

8. $7 \times (108 \div 9) - 4 =$

9. $100 - 15 \times 5 + 10 =$

10. $(148 - 64) \div 4 + 4 =$

11. $3 + 7 \times 7 - 2 =$

12. $6 \times (13 + 12) \div 5 =$

13. $35 \div (5 + 2) - 2 =$

14. $(96 \div 8) + 6 \times 2 =$

Order of Operations

Read and solve each problem. Be careful—some problems have two steps.

1. Hisako wants to buy a new car that costs $21,560. She can trade in her old car for $5,790. How much will be left to pay?

2. Mr. Urbank's car payments are $4,520 a year. If he makes payments for 5 years, how much will he pay for the car?

3. Ms. Wagner bought a used car for $6,844. Tax was another $410. She made a down payment of $2,545. How much was left to pay?

4. Mr. Yan made a down payment of $1,800 on a car that cost $6,453. He paid the rest in 9 equal payments. How much was each payment?

5. Mrs. Zuniga made a down payment of $2,590 on a car. She paid the rest in 8 payments of $593 each. How much did the car cost her?

6. The car Evelyn wants costs $14,972. If she gets the fancier model, it will cost $18,230. How much more does the fancier model cost?

7. Rolando wants a car that costs $19,950. A stereo for it costs $275. If he trades in his old car for $1,500, how much will the new car cost?

8. Ms. Foster made a down payment of $2,800 on a car. Each year for 3 years, she paid $2,931 on the car. How much did the car cost?

Problem Solving: Using the Four Operations

Write the fraction for the shaded part of each whole.

1.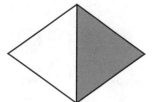
_____

2.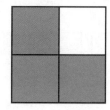
_____

3.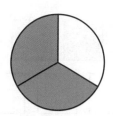
_____

4.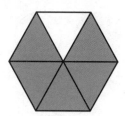
_____

5.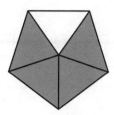
_____

6.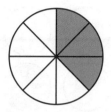
_____

7.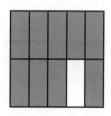
_____

8.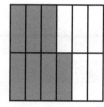
_____

9.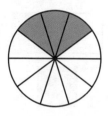
_____

10.
_____

11.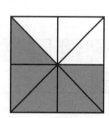
_____

12.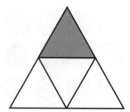
_____

Solve. You can draw a picture to help you.

13. Calvin cut a pie into 8 equal pieces and ate 2 pieces. What part of the pie did he eat?

14. Pearl made lasagna and cut it into 12 equal pieces. There were 3 pieces left over. What part of the lasagna was eaten?

15. Masato cut his birthday cake into 10 equal pieces. He served 9 pieces. What part of the cake was left over?

Fractions: Parts of a Whole

Write the fraction for the shaded part of each set.

1.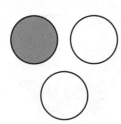

_____

2.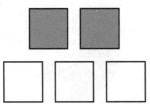

_____

3.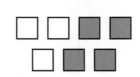

_____

4.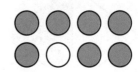

_____

5.

_____

6.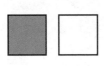

_____

7.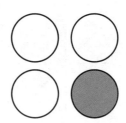

_____

8.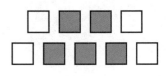

_____

9.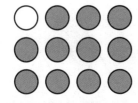

_____

10.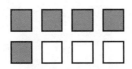

_____

11.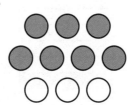

_____

12.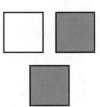

_____

Solve. You can draw a picture to help you.

13. Faith's cat had 6 kittens. There were 4 orange kittens and the rest are tigers. What fraction of the kittens are orange?

14. Haro has 12 tropical fish. Of these, 2 are swordtails. What fraction of his fish are not swordtails?

15. Gwen has 9 birds and 4 of them are canaries. What fraction of her birds are canaries?

Fractions: Parts of a Set

To find a fraction of a number, divide by the **denominator** of the fraction. Then multiply the quotient by the numerator.

$\frac{1}{2}$ of 6 = 3
6 ÷ 2 = 3
1 × 3 = 3

$\frac{2}{3}$ of 12 = 8
12 ÷ 3 = 4
2 × 4 = 8

Find the fraction of each number.

1.

$\frac{1}{3}$ of 12 = _____

2. $\frac{3}{4}$ of 8 = _____

3.

$\frac{4}{5}$ of 10 = _____

4. $\frac{1}{2}$ of 14 = _____

5. $\frac{2}{3}$ of 18 = _____

6. $\frac{1}{4}$ of 12 = _____

7. $\frac{3}{4}$ of 12 = _____

8. $\frac{1}{5}$ of 10 = _____

9. $\frac{5}{8}$ of 16 = _____

10. $\frac{1}{9}$ of 18 = _____

11. $\frac{2}{7}$ of 21 = _____

12. $\frac{1}{3}$ of 15 = _____

13. $\frac{5}{6}$ of 24 = _____

14. $\frac{1}{6}$ of 48 = _____

15. $\frac{2}{5}$ of 20 = _____

Find the sale price of each item. Write it on the tag below the original price.

16. $\frac{1}{2}$ of original price

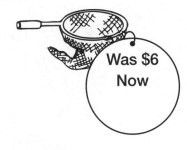

Was $6
Now

17. $\frac{2}{3}$ of original price

Was $15
Now

18. $\frac{4}{5}$ of original price

Was $45
Now

Finding a Fraction of a Set

Equivalent fractions name the same part of a whole in different terms.

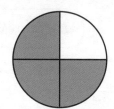 $\frac{3}{4} = \frac{6}{8}$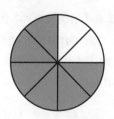

Write equivalent fractions.

1.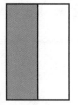

   $\frac{1}{2} = \frac{}{6}$

2.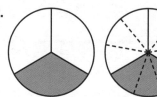

   $\frac{1}{3} = \frac{}{9}$

3.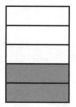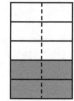

   $\frac{2}{5} = \frac{}{10}$

4.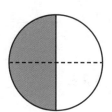

   $\frac{1}{2} = \frac{}{4}$

5.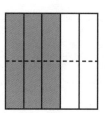

   $\frac{3}{5} = \frac{}{}$

6.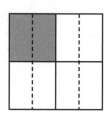

   $\frac{1}{4} = \frac{}{}$

7.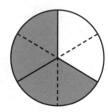

   $\frac{2}{3} = \frac{}{}$

8.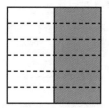

   $\frac{}{2} = \frac{6}{12}$

9.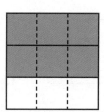

   $\frac{}{} = \frac{6}{9}$

10.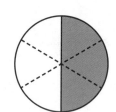

    $\frac{}{} = \frac{3}{6}$

11.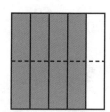

    $\frac{}{} = \frac{8}{10}$

12.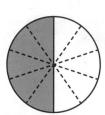

    $\frac{}{2} = \frac{}{10}$

13.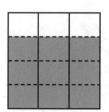

    $\frac{}{} = \frac{}{}$

14.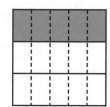

    $\frac{}{} = \frac{}{}$

15.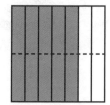

    $\frac{}{} = \frac{}{}$

You can find an equivalent fraction in **higher** terms by multiplying the numerator and the denominator by the same number.

Numerator
↓
$$\frac{1}{3} = \frac{1 \times 2}{3 \times 2} = \frac{2}{6}$$
↑
Denominator

Multiply to find equivalent fractions in higher terms.

1. $\frac{1}{4} = \frac{1 \times 3}{4 \times 3} = \frac{}{12}$
2. $\frac{1}{2} = \frac{1 \times }{2 \times 2} = \frac{}{4}$
3. $\frac{1}{3} = \frac{1 \times }{3 \times } = \frac{}{9}$

4. $\frac{3}{4} = \frac{3 \times }{4 \times } = \frac{}{8}$
5. $\frac{2}{3} = \frac{2 \times }{3 \times } = \frac{}{6}$
6. $\frac{4}{5} = \frac{4 \times }{5 \times } = \frac{}{10}$

7. $\frac{1}{2} = \frac{}{6}$
8. $\frac{1}{4} = \frac{}{8}$
9. $\frac{1}{5} = \frac{}{10}$
10. $\frac{2}{3} = \frac{}{12}$
11. $\frac{1}{2} = \frac{}{8}$

12. $\frac{2}{5} = \frac{}{10}$
13. $\frac{1}{4} = \frac{}{16}$
14. $\frac{1}{6} = \frac{}{12}$
15. $\frac{1}{2} = \frac{}{10}$
16. $\frac{5}{6} = \frac{}{12}$

17. $\frac{2}{3} = \frac{}{9}$
18. $\frac{3}{4} = \frac{}{12}$
19. $\frac{1}{3} = \frac{}{15}$
20. $\frac{3}{5} = \frac{}{20}$
21. $\frac{1}{4} = \frac{}{24}$

Complete each problem with an equivalent fraction in higher terms.

22. The radio weather report said $\frac{3}{5}$ inch of rain fell. The TV report said $\frac{}{10}$ inch fell.

23. The Garcias had $\frac{1}{3}$ foot of water in their basement. They had $\frac{}{12}$ foot of water.

Equivalent Fractions in Higher Terms

Divide the numerator and the denominator by the same number to find a fraction in **lower** terms. A fraction is in **lowest** terms if it can't be divided further.

Lower terms ↓
$$\frac{12}{16} = \frac{12 \div 2}{16 \div 2} = \frac{6}{8}$$

Lowest terms ↓
$$\frac{12}{16} = \frac{12 \div 4}{16 \div 4} = \frac{3}{4}$$

Divide to find equivalent fractions in lower terms.

1. $\frac{4}{8} = \frac{4 \div 2}{8 \div 2} = \frac{\_\_}{4}$
2. $\frac{8}{12} = \frac{8 \div \_\_}{12 \div 2} = \_\_$
3. $\frac{9}{27} = \frac{9 \div \_\_}{27 \div 3} = \_\_$

4. $\frac{6}{12} = \frac{\_\_}{4}$
5. $\frac{12}{16} = \frac{\_\_}{8}$
6. $\frac{18}{24} = \frac{\_\_}{12}$
7. $\frac{10}{20} = \frac{\_\_}{10}$
8. $\frac{6}{18} = \frac{\_\_}{6}$

Divide by the largest possible number to find a fraction in lowest terms.

9. $\frac{16}{24} = \frac{16 \div 8}{24 \div 8} = \frac{\_\_}{3}$
10. $\frac{3}{6} = \frac{3 \div \_\_}{6 \div \_\_} = \frac{\_\_}{2}$
11. $\frac{9}{12} = \frac{9 \div \_\_}{12 \div \_\_} = \frac{\_\_}{4}$

12. $\frac{2}{14} = \frac{\_\_}{7}$
13. $\frac{8}{10} = \frac{\_\_}{5}$
14. $\frac{3}{9} = \frac{\_\_}{3}$
15. $\frac{6}{12} = \frac{\_\_}{2}$
16. $\frac{5}{15} = \frac{\_\_}{3}$

17. $\frac{2}{8} = \_\_$
18. $\frac{4}{12} = \_\_$
19. $\frac{6}{18} = \_\_$
20. $\frac{12}{15} = \_\_$
21. $\frac{18}{24} = \_\_$

Complete each problem with an equivalent fraction in lowest terms.

22. Chef Merang used $\frac{10}{12}$ of a carton of eggs in his famous cake. He used ―— of the eggs.

23. The chef used $\frac{12}{16}$ pound of butter in the buttercream frosting. He used ―— pound of butter.

Equivalent Fractions in Lower Terms

A circle graph shows parts of a whole.

Use the circle graph to answer each question and solve each problem.

TRAIL MIX INGREDIENTS

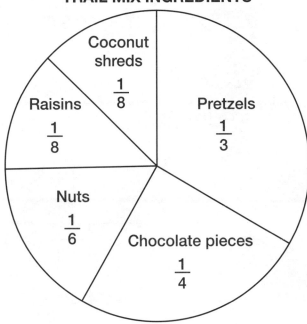

1. How many ingredients are in Trail Mix? _____
2. Which ingredient makes up the largest part of Trail Mix? _____
3. Which ingredient makes up the second largest part? _____
4. What fraction of Trail Mix is nuts?   5. What fraction is raisins?

   _____   _____

6. List the ingredients in order from most to least. _____

7. Is there a greater amount of raisins or nuts in Trail Mix? _____
8. Of which ingredients are there the same amounts? _____

9. If there are 6 cups of Trail Mix, how many cups of nuts are in it?

10. If there are 12 cups of Trail Mix, how many cups of chocolate pieces are in it?

Problem Solving: Using a Circle Graph

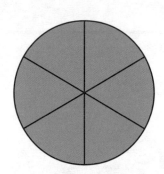 $\frac{6}{6}$ is the same as **1**.

1 is a whole number.

 $\frac{11}{6}$ is the same as $1\frac{5}{6}$.

 $1\frac{5}{6}$ is a mixed number.

Write a whole number or a mixed number for each shaded part.

1.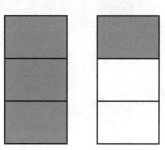

   _____

2.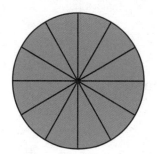

   _____

3.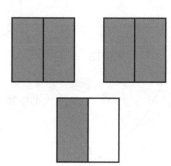

   _____

4.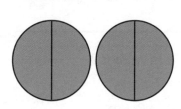

   _____

5.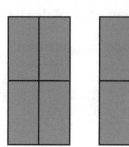

   _____

6.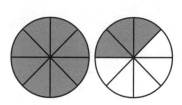

   _____

7.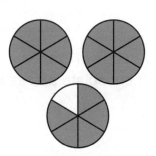

   _____

8.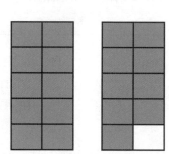

   _____

9.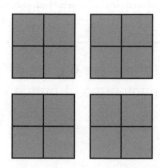

   _____

70

Mixed Numbers

A fraction greater than 1 can be renamed as a whole number or a mixed number.

Divide the numerator by the denominator.
Write the remainder as a fraction.
If the remainder is 0, the answer is a whole number.

$$\frac{9}{4} = 4\overline{)9}^{2\frac{1}{4}}$$
$$\underline{8}$$
$$1$$

Write a whole number or a mixed number for each fraction.

1. $\frac{11}{3} = 3\overline{)11} = 3\frac{2}{3}$
   $\underline{9}$
   2

2. $\frac{15}{4} =$

3. $\frac{11}{2} =$

4. $\frac{8}{5} =$

5. $\frac{8}{4} =$

6. $\frac{15}{5} =$

7. $\frac{17}{6} =$

8. $\frac{22}{7} =$

9. $\frac{20}{9} =$

10. $\frac{16}{8} =$

11. $\frac{19}{3} =$

12. $\frac{35}{7} =$

Find each answer to the problems above in the box. Then write the matching letters in the spaces below to solve the riddle.

CODE

$1\frac{3}{5}$ = M $3\frac{1}{7}$ = H

2 = O $3\frac{2}{3}$ = P

$2\frac{2}{9}$ = R $3\frac{3}{4}$ = L

$2\frac{5}{6}$ = T 5 = K

3 = U $5\frac{1}{2}$ = Y

$6\frac{1}{3}$ = C

What kind of music did the Pilgrims listen to?

__ __ __ __ __ __ __ __
1 2 3 4 5 6 7 8

__ __ __ __
9 10 11 12

Changing Fractions to Mixed Numbers

To compare fractions with like denominators, look at the numerators.

$$\frac{5}{6} > \frac{4}{6}$$

$\frac{5}{6}$ is greater than $\frac{4}{6}$ because 5 is greater than 4.

If the fractions have unlike denominators, first change them to equivalent fractions with like denominators.

$$\frac{1}{3} \bigcirc \frac{3}{6}$$
$$\frac{2}{6} < \frac{3}{6}$$

$\frac{1}{3}$ is less than $\frac{3}{6}$ because $\frac{2}{6}$ is less than $\frac{3}{6}$.

To compare mixed numbers, first look at the whole numbers. Then look at the fractions.

$$2\frac{5}{6} < 3\frac{1}{6}$$

$2\frac{5}{6}$ is less than $3\frac{1}{6}$ because 2 is less than 3.

Compare. Write >, <, or =.

1. $\frac{1}{4} \bigcirc \frac{3}{4}$

2. $\frac{3}{8} \bigcirc \frac{1}{2}$

3. $1\frac{6}{10} \bigcirc 2\frac{1}{10}$

4. $3\frac{3}{5} \bigcirc 2\frac{4}{5}$

5. $\frac{2}{3} \bigcirc \frac{1}{3}$

6. $\frac{5}{10} \bigcirc \frac{1}{2}$

7. $\frac{2}{3} \bigcirc \frac{3}{6}$

8. $7\frac{1}{4} \bigcirc 7\frac{3}{4}$

9. $\frac{5}{8} \bigcirc \frac{7}{8}$

10. $\frac{4}{5} \bigcirc \frac{2}{5}$

11. $4\frac{2}{3} \bigcirc 5\frac{2}{3}$

12. $\frac{1}{4} \bigcirc \frac{1}{8}$

13. $\frac{1}{3} \bigcirc \frac{4}{9}$

14. $\frac{2}{6} \bigcirc \frac{4}{6}$

15. $1\frac{7}{12} \bigcirc 1\frac{5}{12}$

16. $6\frac{1}{5} \bigcirc 6\frac{4}{10}$

17. $\frac{9}{12} \bigcirc \frac{3}{4}$

18. $\frac{7}{10} \bigcirc \frac{6}{10}$

19. Jean walked $\frac{3}{4}$ mile. Paul walked $\frac{4}{8}$ mile. Who walked farther?

20. Kalila ran $2\frac{1}{9}$ miles today. She ran $2\frac{1}{3}$ miles yesterday. On which day did she run farther?

Comparing Fractions and Mixed Numbers

Add fractions with like denominators by adding the numerators.

1.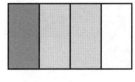
$\frac{1}{4} + \frac{2}{4} = \frac{3}{4}$

2.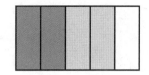
$\frac{2}{5} + \frac{2}{5} = \underline{}$

3.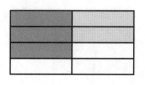
$\frac{3}{8} + \frac{2}{8} = \underline{}$

4. $\frac{2}{9} + \frac{5}{9} = \frac{2+5}{9} = \frac{}{9}$

5. $\frac{4}{6} + \frac{1}{6} = \frac{4+}{6} = \underline{}$

6. $\frac{3}{5} + \frac{1}{5} =$

7. $\frac{2}{7} + \frac{3}{7} =$

8. $\frac{5}{8} + \frac{2}{8} =$

9. $\frac{4}{10} + \frac{3}{10} + \frac{2}{10} =$

10. $\frac{1}{12} + \frac{1}{12} + \frac{3}{12} =$

11. $\frac{6}{15} + \frac{6}{15} + \frac{2}{15} =$

Add. Write each answer in lowest terms.

12. $\frac{5}{12} + \frac{4}{12} = \frac{}{12} = \frac{}{4}$

13. $\frac{3}{16} + \frac{5}{16}$

14. $\frac{3}{8} + \frac{3}{8}$

15. $\frac{2}{9} + \frac{1}{9}$

16. $\frac{7}{10} + \frac{3}{10}$

17. $\frac{2}{6} + \frac{2}{6}$

18. $\frac{4}{7} + \frac{3}{7}$

19. $\frac{2}{12} + \frac{4}{12}$

20. $\frac{2}{14} + \frac{0}{14}$

21. $\frac{9}{18} + \frac{3}{18}$

22. Nick spent $\frac{1}{8}$ of his allowance on comic books and $\frac{3}{8}$ on a car model. What part did he spend?

23. LaToya earns $\frac{4}{16}$ of her allowance mowing the lawn and $\frac{8}{16}$ washing dishes. What part does she earn?

Adding Fractions with Like Denominators

Subtract fractions with like denominators by subtracting the numerators.

1.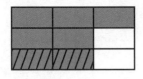
$\frac{7}{9} - \frac{2}{9} = \frac{5}{9}$

2.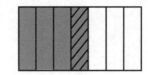
$\frac{4}{7} - \frac{1}{7} = \frac{}{}$

3.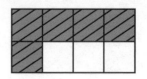
$\frac{5}{8} - \frac{5}{8} = \frac{}{}$

4. $\frac{3}{5} - \frac{1}{5} = \frac{3-1}{5} = \frac{}{5}$

5. $\frac{5}{10} - \frac{2}{10} = \frac{5-}{10} = \frac{}{}$

6. $\frac{3}{4} - \frac{2}{4} =$

7. $\frac{7}{8} - \frac{4}{8} =$

8. $\frac{11}{12} - \frac{4}{12} =$

9. $\frac{2}{3} - \frac{1}{3} =$

10. $\frac{8}{9} - \frac{6}{9} =$

11. $\frac{15}{18} - \frac{8}{18} =$

Subtract. Write each answer in lowest terms.

12. $\frac{7}{9} - \frac{4}{9} = \frac{}{9} = \frac{}{3}$

13. $\frac{5}{8} - \frac{1}{8}$

14. $\frac{11}{12} - \frac{3}{12}$

15. $\frac{2}{6} - \frac{0}{6}$

16. $\frac{9}{10} - \frac{5}{10}$

17. $\frac{4}{7} - \frac{4}{7}$

18. $\frac{15}{16} - \frac{12}{16}$

19. $\frac{13}{15} - \frac{8}{15}$

20. $\frac{10}{12} - \frac{1}{12}$

21. $\frac{20}{24} - \frac{14}{24}$

22. There was $\frac{3}{10}$ of an apple pie left. Travis had $\frac{1}{10}$ of the pie for lunch. How much of the pie is left now?

23. There was $\frac{7}{12}$ quart of milk in the refrigerator. How much will be left if Cheryl drinks $\frac{3}{12}$ quart?

To add fractions with unlike denominators, first change them to equivalent fractions with **like** denominators. Then add.

$$\frac{3}{8} = \frac{3}{8}$$
$$+\frac{1}{4} = \frac{2}{8}$$
$$\overline{\frac{5}{8}}$$

$$\frac{2}{3} = \frac{10}{15}$$
$$+\frac{1}{5} = \frac{3}{15}$$
$$\overline{\frac{13}{15}}$$

Find equivalent fractions. Then add. Write the answer in lowest terms.

1. $\frac{1}{2} =$
  $+\frac{2}{8} =$ _____

2. $\frac{1}{3}$
  $+\frac{2}{9}$

3. $\frac{2}{6}$
  $+\frac{1}{2}$

4. $\frac{5}{8}$
  $+\frac{3}{16}$

5. $\frac{2}{3}$
  $+\frac{1}{12}$

6. $\frac{1}{2}$
  $+\frac{3}{10}$

7. $\frac{1}{4}$
  $+\frac{5}{12}$

8. $\frac{2}{5}$
  $+\frac{1}{10}$

9. $\frac{2}{6}$
  $+\frac{1}{3}$

10. $\frac{5}{14}$
  $+\frac{3}{7}$

11. $\frac{7}{15}$
  $+\frac{2}{5}$

12. $\frac{1}{3}$
  $+\frac{3}{5}$

13. $\frac{5}{6}$
  $+\frac{1}{18}$

14. $\frac{7}{24}$
  $+\frac{1}{8}$

15. $\frac{2}{9}$
  $+\frac{1}{6}$

16. $\frac{3}{8}$
  $+\frac{7}{12}$

17. Mr. Fung has $\frac{1}{4}$ pound of worms and $\frac{1}{2}$ pound of other bait. How much bait does he have in all?

18. Of Erica's catch, $\frac{1}{4}$ was bass and $\frac{1}{3}$ was perch. What part of Erica's catch was bass and perch?

Adding Fractions with Unlike Denominators

To subtract fractions with unlike denominators, first change them to equivalent fractions with **like** denominators. Then subtract.

$$\frac{5}{6} = \frac{5}{6}$$
$$-\frac{2}{3} = \frac{4}{6}$$
$$\overline{\frac{1}{6}}$$

$$\frac{3}{4} = \frac{9}{12}$$
$$-\frac{1}{3} = \frac{4}{12}$$
$$\overline{\frac{5}{12}}$$

Find equivalent fractions. Then subtract. Write the answer in lowest terms.

1. $\frac{1}{2} =$
    $-\frac{1}{10} =$ _____

2. $\frac{5}{9}$
    $-\frac{1}{3}$

3. $\frac{3}{4}$
    $-\frac{1}{8}$

4. $\frac{11}{12}$
    $-\frac{3}{4}$

5. $\frac{7}{10}$
    $-\frac{1}{2}$

6. $\frac{5}{6}$
    $-\frac{1}{3}$

7. $\frac{4}{5}$
    $-\frac{3}{10}$

8. $\frac{2}{3}$
    $-\frac{5}{12}$

9. $\frac{13}{18}$
    $-\frac{1}{6}$

10. $\frac{5}{6}$
    $-\frac{7}{9}$

11. $\frac{2}{3}$
    $-\frac{8}{15}$

12. $\frac{9}{10}$
    $-\frac{1}{2}$

13. $\frac{4}{5}$
    $-\frac{2}{3}$

14. $\frac{17}{21}$
    $-\frac{2}{7}$

15. $\frac{5}{7}$
    $-\frac{1}{3}$

16. $\frac{3}{4}$
    $-\frac{2}{5}$

17. Omar had $\frac{7}{8}$ of a bag of plant food. He used $\frac{1}{2}$ bag. How much was left?

18. Ms. Linden's garden is $\frac{4}{5}$ acre big and $\frac{1}{4}$ acre is planted in potatoes. What part is planted with other things?

76 Subtracting Fractions with Unlike Denominators

To add or subtract mixed numbers, first work with the fractions. Then work with the whole numbers.

$3\frac{1}{8}$
$+2\frac{2}{8}$
$\overline{\frac{3}{8}}$

$3\frac{1}{8}$
$+2\frac{2}{8}$
$\overline{5\frac{3}{8}}$

$9\frac{4}{5}$
$-2\frac{1}{5}$
$\overline{\frac{3}{5}}$

$9\frac{4}{5}$
$-2\frac{1}{5}$
$\overline{7\frac{3}{5}}$

Add or subtract. Write each answer in lowest terms.

1. $3\frac{1}{3}$
   $+1\frac{1}{3}$

2. $3\frac{1}{2}$
   $-2\frac{1}{2}$

3. $5\frac{1}{4}$
   $+3\frac{2}{4}$

4. $9\frac{7}{8}$
   $-3\frac{3}{8}$

5. $8\frac{5}{6}$
   $-5\frac{1}{6}$

6. $7\frac{3}{5}$
   $-1\frac{2}{5}$

7. $3\frac{3}{8}$
   $+2\frac{2}{8}$

8. $6\frac{2}{9}$
   $+2\frac{4}{9}$

9. $2\frac{1}{10}$
   $+4\frac{1}{10}$

10. $8\frac{3}{4}$
    $-7\frac{1}{4}$

11. $4\frac{2}{5}$
    $+1\frac{2}{5}$

12. $9\frac{11}{12}$
    $-5\frac{5}{12}$

13. $3\frac{8}{9}$
    $-1\frac{5}{9}$

14. $2\frac{1}{6}$
    $+7\frac{3}{6}$

15. $5\frac{5}{12}$
    $-3\frac{4}{12}$

16. $8\frac{9}{10}$
    $-5\frac{7}{10}$

17. Jamal mixed $1\frac{1}{4}$ cans of blue paint with $1\frac{3}{4}$ cans of yellow paint. How much paint did he have then?

18. Stacey had $5\frac{7}{8}$ yards of cloth. She used $4\frac{5}{8}$ yards to make a curtain. How much cloth was left?

Adding and Subtracting Mixed Numbers

Read and solve each problem. Write each answer in lowest terms.

1. The Villas traveled $\frac{1}{3}$ of the way in the morning and $\frac{1}{6}$ of the way in the afternoon. What part did they travel that day?

2. The gas tank held $12\frac{7}{8}$ gallons when the Villas left. There were $4\frac{1}{8}$ gallons in it when they stopped for lunch. How much gas did they use?

3. The Villas spent $\frac{7}{12}$ of their vacation at Sea Beach and $\frac{5}{12}$ of it on Neva Island. How much more time did they spend at Sea Beach?

4. Marcos spent $\frac{1}{4}$ of his money on souvenirs and $\frac{1}{5}$ on snacks. What part of his money did he spend?

5. About $\frac{3}{16}$ of the people camping at Sea Beach are from Virginia and $\frac{3}{8}$ are from Maryland. What part are from these two states?

6. Of Rosa's shell collection, $\frac{1}{3}$ came from Sea Beach and $\frac{1}{7}$ came from Neva Island. What part came from these two places?

7. Rosa read $3\frac{3}{12}$ books on the trip. Marcos read $2\frac{7}{12}$ books. How many books did they read in all?

8. Mrs. Villa drove $\frac{1}{6}$ of the way home. Mr. Villa drove $\frac{4}{9}$ of the way. How much more did Mr. Villa drive?

78   Problem Solving: Using Fractions and Mixed Numbers

A **ratio** is a way to compare two numbers.

There are 2 boys and 3 girls helping to plan a class party.

The ratio of boys to girls is 2 to 3, or $\frac{2}{3}$.

The ratio of girls to boys is 3 to 2, or $\frac{3}{2}$.

Write a fraction for each ratio.

1. 1 slice of cake to 2 scoops of ice cream

2. 2 straws to 1 drink

3. 1 bag of chips to 6 students

4. 1 pizza to 8 students

5. 3 napkins to 2 students

6. 1 cup to 1 student

7. 3 cupcakes to 4 cookies

8. 6 gumdrops to 1 bag of candy

9. 5 cans of cola to 2 cans of grape soda

10. 1 table to 4 students

11. 4 chairs to 1 table

12. 2 trays of ice cubes to 5 bottles of juice

13. The students hung 9 green balloons and 12 purple balloons. What is the ratio of green balloons to purple balloons?

14. What is the ratio of purple balloons to green balloons?

15. What is the ratio of green balloons to the total number of balloons?

16. What is the ratio of purple balloons to the total number of balloons?

Ratios

Probability is the chance of something happening.

There are 2 possible outcomes to flipping a coin, heads or tails.

The probability that the coin will land on heads is 1 out of 2. Another way to write probability is as a fraction:

$\dfrac{1}{2}$ ← Number of heads
← Number of ways the coin can land

Write a fraction for each probability.

What is the probability of the spinner stopping on—

1. the letter X?
2. a purple space?

3. a letter?
4. a number?

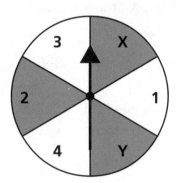

In the bowl are 3 black marbles, 3 white marbles, and 2 gray marbles. If you pick a marble without looking, what is the probability of getting—

5. a black marble?
6. a white marble?

7. a gray marble?
8. a white or a black marble?

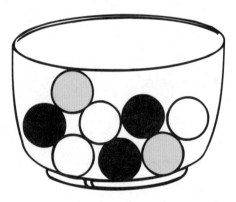

There are 10 cards. If they are shuffled and you pick one without looking, what is the probability of getting—

9. a star?
10. a circle?

11. a black circle?
12. a white star?

Some problems can be solved by making a **tree diagram**.

Akira is wrapping a present. He can use striped paper or dotted paper. He can use red, blue, or green ribbon. How many different ways can Akira wrap the present?

The tree diagram shows that Akira can wrap it 6 different ways.

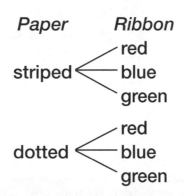

Make a tree diagram to solve each problem.

1. Lawrence has red pants and blue pants. He has a yellow shirt and a green shirt. How many different outfits can he make?

2. A restaurant offers a soup-and-sandwich special for lunch. Juanita has a choice of tomato or vegetable soup. For a sandwich, she can pick from chicken, tuna, or egg salad. How many different lunches could she have?

3. On a rainy afternoon, Dominic and Will decided to play a game and then watch a movie. They can play cards, chess, or checkers. They can watch *Star Battle*, *Saddle Trek*, or *Mystery Voyage*. How many ways can Dominic and Will spend the afternoon?

Problem Solving: Making a Tree Diagram

You can write tenths as a fraction or as a decimal.
This is three tenths.

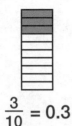

$\frac{3}{10} = 0.3$

A decimal point separates the ones and the tenths.
This is two and one tenth.

$2\frac{1}{10} = 2.1$

Write a fraction or mixed number and a decimal to show how much is shaded.

1. 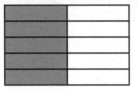 $\frac{5}{10} = 0.5$

2. 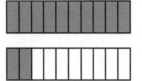   ___ = ___

3. 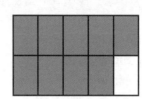   ___ = ___

4.   ___ = ___

5. 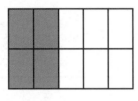   ___ = ___

6. 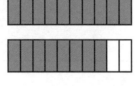   ___ = ___

7. ___ = ___

8. ___ = ___

Write a decimal for each number name.

9. five and seven tenths ___5.7___

10. nine tenths _____

11. six and one tenth _____

12. seven tenths _____

13. four tenths _____

14. twenty and one tenth _____

15. ten and eight tenths _____

16. two and five tenths _____

17. four and two tenths _____

18. six tenths _____

Write a decimal for each fraction.

19. Axel ate $\frac{4}{10}$ kilogram of dog food. _____

20. Niesha is $1\frac{5}{10}$ meters tall. _____

21. Mr. Welch filled his gas tank with $26\frac{7}{10}$ liters of gas. _____

Decimals: Tenths

You can write hundredths as a fraction or as a decimal. This is twenty-five hundredths.

$\frac{25}{100} = 0.25$

Write a fraction and a decimal to show how much is shaded.

1.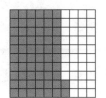
2.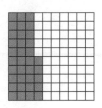
3.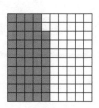
4.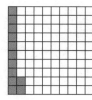

$\frac{62}{100}$ = 0.62   ___ = ___   ___ = ___   ___ = ___

5.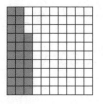
6.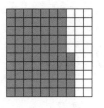
7.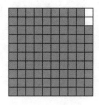
8.

___ = ___   ___ = ___   ___ = ___   ___ = ___

Write a decimal for each number name.

9. four and seven hundredths   4.07

10. two and eighty-nine hundredths   _____

11. seven and seventy-five hundredths   _____

12. ten and forty-six hundredths   _____

13. ninety-nine hundredths   _____

Write a decimal for each fraction.

14. Natasha jogs $1\frac{66}{100}$ miles each day.   _____

15. The car used only $2\frac{19}{100}$ gallons of gas.   _____

16. There were $5\frac{7}{100}$ pounds of sugar left.   _____

Decimals: Hundredths

To compare decimals, compare the digits in the same places.

Compare tenths to tenths, hundredths to hundredths, and whole numbers to whole numbers.

2.15 < 2.92

Compare. Write >, <, or =.

1. 0.8 ◯ 0.3
2. 1.6 ◯ 0.7
3. 2.4 ◯ 4.2
4. 5.0 ◯ 0.5
5. 2.1 ◯ 2.10
6. 8.9 ◯ 9.1
7. 3.6 ◯ 3.60
8. 1.83 ◯ 2.38
9. 2.00 ◯ 1.99
10. 4.67 ◯ 4.76
11. 6.9 ◯ 6.09
12. 9.01 ◯ 9.10
13. 7.21 ◯ 8.01
14. 8.03 ◯ 3.08
15. 1.50 ◯ 1.05
16. 9.2 ◯ 9.20
17. 4.67 ◯ 4.7
18. 3.8 ◯ 8.03

Read the trail signs below. Then write the names of the trails and their lengths in order from shortest to longest.

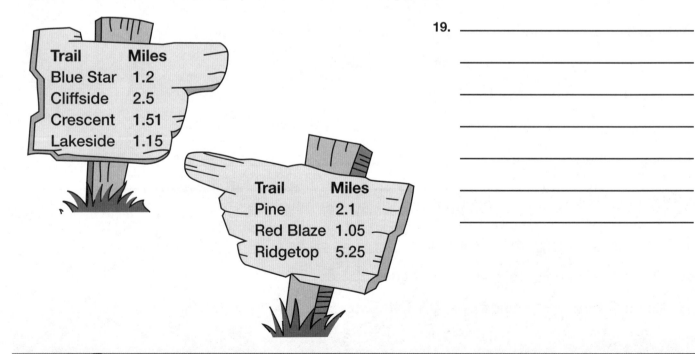

19. _____

Comparing and Ordering Decimals

Add decimals the same way you add whole numbers. Be sure the decimal points line up. Put the decimal point in the answer in the same place.

Add. Line up the decimal point in the answer.

1. 0.5
  +0.2

2. 0.4
  +0.4

3. 0.7
  +0.8

```
  0.88       5.16
+ 0.11     + 2.97
  0.99       8.13
```

4. 5.4
  +2.7

5. 1.8
  +3.6

6. 2.4
  +8.7

7. 0.16
  +0.32

8. 0.68
  +0.19

9. 4.20
  +2.78

10. 5.06
  +1.99

11. 2.43
  +2.67

12. 52.4
  +29.7

13. 89.2
  +80.9

14. 1.65
  +4.47

15. 9.39
  +3.84

16. 4.78
  +5.37

17. 35.4
  +75.9

18. 6.17
  +3.46

19. 73.8
  +89.4

20. 57.9
  +69.9

21. 8.35
  +2.65

22. The Bancrofts sailed 26.8 kilometers to Peele Island and then 16.6 kilometers to Greenlay Island. How far did they sail altogether?

23. The boat used 9.33 liters of gas this morning and 8.25 liters this afternoon. How much gas did it use today?

Adding Decimals

Subtract decimals the same way you subtract whole numbers. Regroup if necessary. Remember to line up the decimal points.

Subtract. Watch the decimal points.

1. 0.8
   −0.3

2. 0.9
   −0.1

3. 0.6
   −0.5

```
   6.0        7.45
  −2.5       −2.36
   ───        ────
   3.5        5.09
```

4. 7.8
   −2.5

5. 8.1
   −1.9

6. 5.0
   −3.1

7. 0.79
   −0.32

8. 0.46
   −0.17

9. 9.37
   −4.35

10. 8.12
   −2.26

11. 3.58
   −1.59

12. 62.3
   −34.7

13. 26.7
   −17.9

14. 8.14
   −2.58

15. 5.36
   −4.49

16. 9.02
   −5.93

17. 81.2
   −14.8

18. 4.73
   −2.86

19. 35.2
   −16.5

20. 92.4
   −82.9

21. 6.40
   −3.53

22. Derek's biggest rabbit weighs 9.98 pounds. His smallest rabbit weighs 2.25 pounds. How much less does the smallest rabbit weigh?

23. A bag held 60.5 pounds of rabbit food. Derek used 15.9 pounds of it. How much food is left now?

When you add or subtract decimals with different numbers of places, be sure to line up the decimal points. Write zeros to help you.

```
  54.46        82.90
+  1.30      -  5.48
  55.76        77.42
```

Add or subtract. Write zeros where necessary. Watch the signs.

1.   8.39
   +10.6

2.   9.14
    −2.3

3.   78.5
   −68.74

4.   2.7
   +8.45

5.   0.46
   +3.6

6.   5.07
    −0.6

7.   13.8
   +17.54

8.   6.13
    −1.7

9.   39.92
   + 7.3

10.   4.1
    −0.25

Rewrite each problem in vertical form. Then solve.

11. 2.76 + 38.4 =

12. 67.1 − 0.79 =

13. 4.3 + 2.86 + 87.1 =

14. 8.2 − 3.96 =

15. 3.4 + 28.9 + 4.05 =

16. 53.1 − 38.09 =

Solve.

17. Elaine carried 8.24 pounds of food on her safari. She ate 2.3 pounds of it on the first day. How much did she have to carry then?

18. In three days, Elaine hiked 4.2, 6.07, and 9.83 miles. How far did she hike in all?

Adding and Subtracting Decimals

Mr. Elliot teaches people how to find and prepare wild foods. Today, his class collected 4.5 pounds of cattail buds. The students cooked and ate 3.75 pounds of them. How much was left?

To add or subtract decimals, be sure to line up the decimal points first.

```
  4.5
 -3.75
  0.75 pound
```

Read and solve each problem. Be sure to check your answer.

1. Donna collected 2.25 pounds of wild grapes. Nobu collected 1.79 pounds of them. How much did they gather altogether?

2. Aiko used 1.97 pounds of sugar to make wild strawberry jam. The recipe called for only 1.75 pounds. How much more did Aiko use?

3. The students picked 2.59 pounds of dandelion greens. After cleaning, only 2.05 pounds were left. How much was thrown away?

4. Luis ground 0.4 pound of acorn flour. Veronica made 0.47 pound of flour. How much flour did they grind in all?

5. Last winter, Mr. Elliot made 0.8 gallon of maple syrup. He has used 0.56 gallon so far this year. How much does he have left?

6. Melody and Rita made 5.5 quarts of birch tea. They drank 0.63 quart of it. How much was left?

7. Pablo brought back 3.56 pounds of blackberries. He had eaten 0.44 pound of berries while picking. How much had he picked?

8. Mr. Elliot caught a 1.7-pound trout. Leticia caught a 0.98-pound trout. How much did the two fish weigh together?

Problem Solving: Using Decimals

A **centimeter** (cm) is a unit of length in the metric system.

This fishhook is about 5 centimeters long.

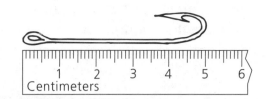

Measure each numbered item in the fish tank to the nearest centimeter.

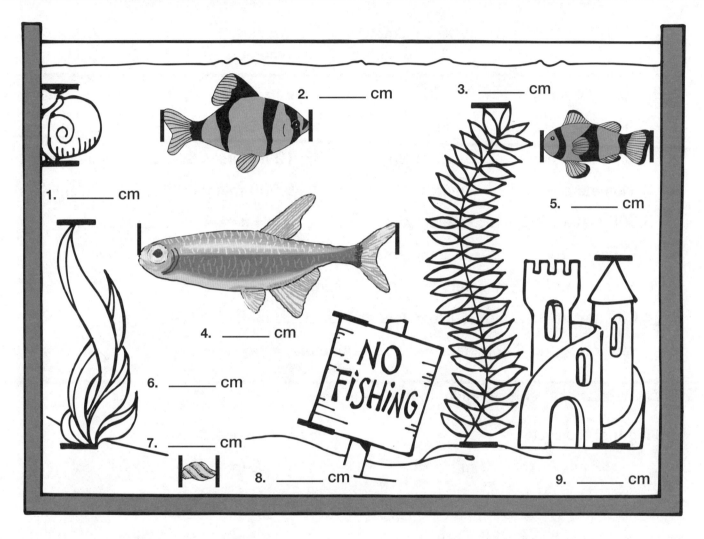

10. The fish tank is _____ centimeters long and _____ centimeters high.

Measure these things to the nearest centimeter.

11. the length of your nose _____ cm
12. the width of your hand _____ cm
13. the length of your ear _____ cm
14. the width of your thumb _____ cm
15. the length of your foot _____ cm

16. the length of a pencil _____ cm
17. the width of a math book _____ cm
18. the length of a tablet _____ cm
19. the width of an eraser _____ cm
20. the length of a desk _____ cm

Measurement: Centimeter

89

The **meter** (m) is the basic metric unit for measuring length. A baseball bat is about 1 meter long.

The **kilometer** (km) is used for measuring long distances.

100 centimeters = 1 meter
1,000 meters = 1 kilometer

Complete.

1. 4 meters = _____ centimeters
2. 500 centimeters = _____ meters
3. 700 centimeters = _____ meters
4. 12 meters = _____ centimeters
5. 2 kilometers = _____ meters
6. 5,000 meters = _____ kilometers
7. 8,000 meters = _____ kilometers
8. 9 kilometers = _____ meters
9. 260 centimeters = _____ meters and _____ centimeters
10. 8 meters and 35 centimeters = _____ centimeters
11. 4,600 meters = _____ kilometers and _____ meters
12. 7 kilometers and 400 meters = _____ meters

Circle the best answer for the length of each item.

13. length of a bicycle
    2 cm   or   2 m

14. height of a door
    2 m   or   2 km

15. distance run in an hour
    6 m   or   6 km

16. length of a teaspoon
    15 cm   or   15 m

17. width of a door
    1 m   or   5 m

18. distance between cities
    12 m   or   12 km

19. distance driven in an hour
    10 km   or   100 km

20. length of a car
    4 m   or   40 m

21. an adult's height
    1 m   or   2 m

22. length of a park
    5 m   or   5 km

Measurement: Metric Units of Length

An eyedropper holds about
1 milliliter (mL).

A pitcher holds about
1 liter (L).

1,000 milliliters = **1** liter

Circle the unit you would use to measure each item.

1.
   mL   L

2.
   mL   L

3.
   mL   L

4.
   mL   L

Circle the best answer for each amount.

5.
   1 mL   100 mL

6.
   25 mL   250 mL

7.
   5 mL   500 mL

8.
   3 mL   30 mL

9.
   1 L   100 L

10.
    10 L   100 L

11.
    15 L   150 L

12.
    1 L   10 L

Solve.

13. Duncan opened a 1-liter carton of milk. He drank 250 milliliters of it. How much milk was left in the carton?

14. Hatsu gave her plants 675 milliliters of water on Monday, 580 on Wednesday, and 745 on Saturday. How many liters of water was that?

Measurement: Milliliter and Liter

A bean has a mass of about 1 **gram** (g).

Two loaves of bread have a mass of about 1 **kilogram** (kg).

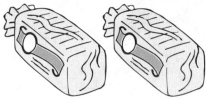

1,000 grams = 1 kilogram

Circle the unit you would use to measure each item.

1.

g   kg

2.

g   kg

3.

g   kg

4.

g   kg

Circle the best answer for the mass of each item.

5.

10 g   100 g

6.

20 g   200 g

7.

3 g   300 g

8.

50 g   500 g

9.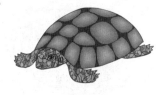

1 kg   10 kg

10.

5 kg   50 kg

11.

8 kg   80 kg

12.

10 kg   100 kg

Solve.

13. Mr. Morgan bought 1 kilogram of cheese. He used 400 grams of it in sandwiches. How much cheese was left?

14. Daphne has 2 packs of dog food. Each one has a mass of 1,500 grams. How many kilograms of dog food does she have?

Measurement: Gram and Kilogram

You can measure temperature in **degrees Celsius** (°C).

Write the temperature shown on each thermometer.

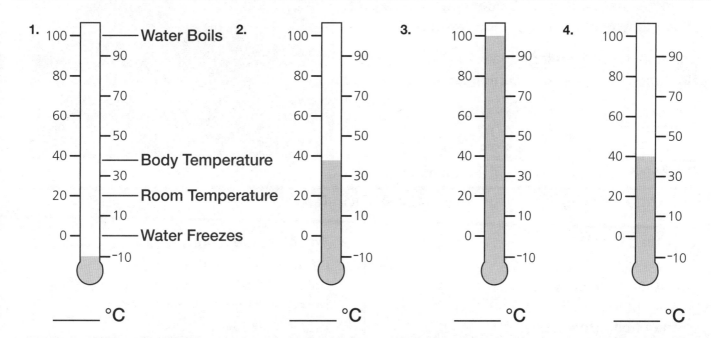

Match each temperature above to the correct picture below.

Shade each thermometer to show the given temperature. Then circle the word that best describes that temperature.

9. 0°C   10. 20°C   11. 40°C   12. 10°C

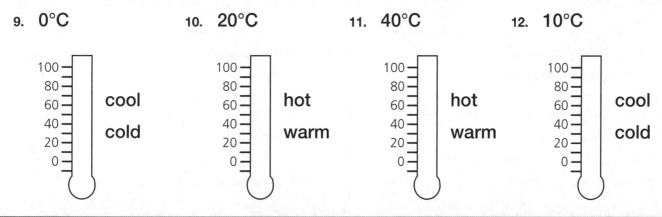

Measurement: Degrees Celsius

Some problems contain hidden information.

Mrs. Kemp had 4 meters of cloth. She cut off 4 pieces that were each 82 centimeters long. How many centimeters of cloth were left?

You know that 1 meter equals 100 centimeters. So 4 meters equals 400 centimeters.

First, multiply.
```
  82
×  4
 328
```
328 centimeters

Then subtract.
```
 400
-328
  72
```
72 centimeters

Read and solve each problem below. Check each answer.

1. A road lies 850 meters west of the Kemps' cabin. A lake lies 150 meters east of the cabin. How many kilometers apart are the road and the lake?

2. Wayne made 2 liters of iced tea for 4 people. If each person drinks an equal amount, how many milliliters can each person have?

3. Peaceful Lake is 3 kilometers long and 750 meters wide. How much longer than wide is the lake?

4. Amber put 200 grams of birdseed in each of 5 feeders. How many kilograms of birdseed did she use in all?

5. Mr. Kemp had 2 meters of cord. He cut it into 5 pieces of equal length. How many centimeters long was each piece?

6. Mrs. Kemp filled a lamp with oil from a full 1-liter bottle. If 625 milliliters of oil were left in the bottle, how much did she put in the lamp?

7. The Kemps picked 3 kilograms of berries. They ate 800 grams of berries and made the rest into jam. How many grams of berries did they use for jam?

8. The Kemps walked 275 meters east, 970 meters south, and 755 meters east again on a trail. How many kilometers did they walk?

Problem Solving: Using Hidden Information

An **inch** (in.) is a unit of length.

The length of this bolt to the nearest—

　inch is 3 inches

　half inch is $2\frac{1}{2}$ inches

　quarter inch is $2\frac{3}{4}$ inches

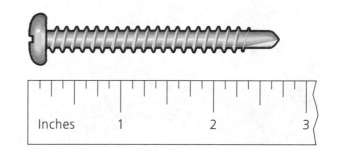

Measure each item on the tool board to the nearest inch, half inch, or quarter inch.

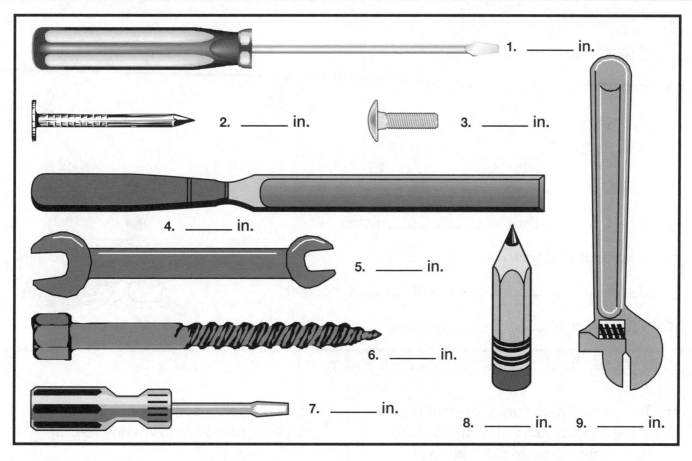

1. _____ in.
2. _____ in.
3. _____ in.
4. _____ in.
5. _____ in.
6. _____ in.
7. _____ in.
8. _____ in.
9. _____ in.

10. The tool board is _____ inches long and _____ inches high.

Measure these things to the nearest inch, half inch, or quarter inch.

11. the length of your desk _____ in.
12. the width of your desk _____ in.
13. the height of your desk _____ in.
14. the length of your shoe _____ in.
15. the width of your shoe _____ in.
16. the height of your chair _____ in.
17. the length of your pencil _____ in.
18. the width of a math book _____ in.
19. the height of your knee _____ in.
20. the length of your arm _____ in.

Measurement: Inch, Half Inch, Quarter Inch

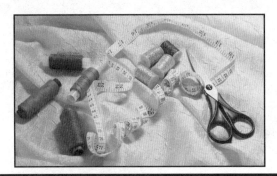

12 inches = 1 foot (ft)
3 feet = 1 yard (yd)
36 inches = 1 yard
5,280 feet = 1 mile (mi)
1,760 yards = 1 mile

Complete.

1. 4 feet = _____ inches
2. 6 feet = _____ yards
3. 2 yards = _____ inches
4. 2 miles = _____ feet
5. 12 feet = _____ yards
6. 1,760 yards = _____ mile
7. 2 feet and 6 inches = _____ inches
8. 7 yards and 2 feet = _____ feet
9. 8 feet = _____ yards and _____ feet
10. 7,280 feet = _____ mile and _____ feet

Solve. Be careful—some problems have two steps.

11. This year, 2 miles of cloth were used to make suits at Zoot Clothing Factory. How many yards of cloth is that?

12. Mrs. Angelo's suit was made with 5 yards of cloth. How many feet of cloth was that?

13. Ed Zoot made a pair of pants that were 42 inches long. How many feet and inches long were the pants?

14. There are 30 feet of cloth left on a roll. A jacket takes 2 yards of cloth. How many jackets can be made with the cloth left on the roll?

Measurement: Customary Units of Length

2 cups (c) = 1 pint (pt)
2 pints = 1 quart (qt)
4 quarts = 1 gallon (gal)

Complete.

1. 3 gallons = _____ quarts
2. 2 quarts = _____ pints
3. 16 quarts = _____ gallons
4. 6 pints = _____ cups
5. 2 gallons = _____ quarts
6. 5 quarts = _____ pints
7. 10 cups = _____ pints
8. 26 pints = _____ quarts
9. 1 gallon = _____ pints
10. 8 cups = _____ quarts

16 ounces (oz) = 1 pound (lb)

Complete.

11. $\frac{1}{4}$ pound = _____ ounces
12. 2 pounds = _____ ounces
13. 48 ounces = _____ pounds
14. 8 ounces = _____ pound
15. 36 ounces = _____ pounds and _____ ounces
16. 5 pounds = _____ ounces

Solve.

17. Bruce has a 1-pound box of soap powder. He uses 4 ounces to wash clothes. How much is left?

18. Alyssa mixed 2 quarts of orange juice and 6 quarts of lemonade. How many gallons of punch did she make?

19. Deion uses 8 ounces of chocolate in a cake. If he bakes 2 cakes, how much chocolate will he need?

20. Sydney picked 18 pints of strawberries. How many quarts is that?

Measurement: Customary Units of Capacity and Weight

You can measure temperature in **degrees Fahrenheit** (°F).

Write the temperature shown on each thermometer.

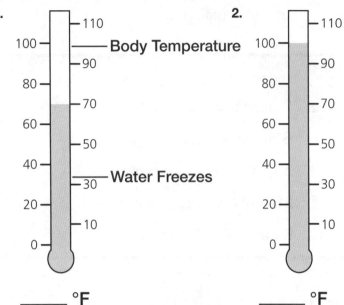 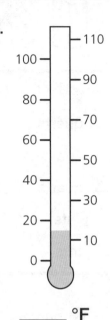 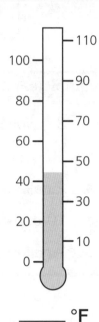

1. _____ °F
2. _____ °F
3. _____ °F
4. _____ °F

Now match each temperature above to the correct picture below.

5. _____ °F
6. _____ °F
7. _____ °F
8. _____ °F

Solve. Write each answer in degrees Fahrenheit (°F).

9. Water boils at 212°F. It freezes at 32°F. How much greater is the temperature at which it boils?

10. The oven temperature is 275°F. It needs to be 350°F to bake cookies. How many degrees should it be turned up?

11. The temperature at dawn was 42°F. By noon, it had risen 45 degrees. What was the temperature then?

12. Taro's temperature is normally 98°F. When he was sick, it went up 5 degrees. What was his temperature then?

Measurement: Degrees Fahrenheit

A line graph shows change over time.

Use this line graph to answer each question and solve each problem below.

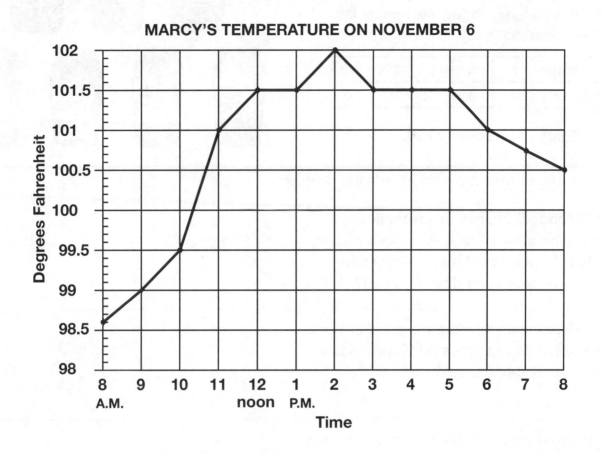

1. What is recorded on this line graph? _____

2. How often was Marcy's temperature taken? _____

3. What part of a degree do the short lines between numbers stand for? _____

4. At 8 A.M., Marcy's temperature was 98.6°F, or normal. What was her temperature two hours later? _____

5. At what time was Marcy's temperature highest? _____

6. What was her highest temperature? _____

7. How many degrees did Marcy's temperature drop between 2 P.M. and 8 P.M.?

8. How much higher was her temperature at 8 P.M. than at 8 A.M.?

Problem Solving: Using a Line Graph

99

© The Continental Press, Inc. DUPLICATING THIS MATERIAL IS ILLEGAL.

Some problems can be solved by making a table.

For every 3 jars of grape jelly it sells, the farm market sells 4 jars of strawberry jam. If it sold 15 jars of grape jelly today, how many jars of strawberry jam did it sell?

grape	3	6	9	12	15
strawberry	4	8	12	16	20

It sold 20 jars of strawberry jam.

Make a table to find the answer to each problem.

1. Mr. Vo adds 2 ounces of seasoning to every 5 pounds of meat to make sausage. He has 25 pounds of meat. How many ounces of seasoning does he need?

2. Ms. Wilson sells 3 pies for every 2 cakes at her bakery. Today, she sold 27 pies. How many cakes did she sell?

3. A clean-up crew picked up 7 bags of trash for every 2 miles of highway. If the crew picked up 49 bags of trash today, how many miles of highway did they clean up?

4. For every 12 apples Toby picks, 2 apples are bad. How many apples can he expect to be bad if he picks 60 apples?

5. A store gives $3 to a charity for every $25 a customer spends. How much would the store give to the charity if the customer spends $100?

6. Shelby changes the oil in her car every 3,000 miles. She uses 5 quarts of oil each time. If she drove 15,000 miles this year, how many quarts of oil did she use?

Problem Solving: Making a Table

A **line** is a straight path with no endpoints. It is named by any two points on it. This line is $\overleftrightarrow{AB}$ or $\overleftrightarrow{BA}$.

A **line segment** is part of a line between two points. It is named by its endpoints. This line segment is $\overline{CD}$ or $\overline{DC}$.

Name each line and line segment two ways.

1.  _____

2. 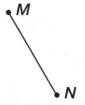 _____

3. 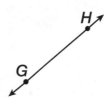 _____

4.  _____

5.   _____

6. 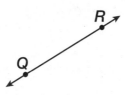 _____

7.  _____

8.  _____

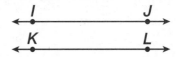

Intersecting lines meet at a point. $\overleftrightarrow{EF}$ and $\overleftrightarrow{GH}$ are intersecting lines.

Parallel lines never meet. They are always the same distance apart. $\overleftrightarrow{IJ}$ and $\overleftrightarrow{KL}$ are parallel lines.

Write *intersecting* or *parallel* to describe each pair of lines.

9. 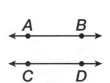 _____

10. 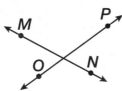 _____

11. 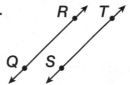 _____

12. 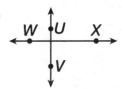 _____

13. 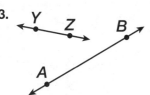 _____

14.   _____

15. 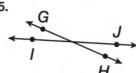 _____

16. 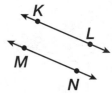 _____

Geometry: Lines and Line Segments

A **ray** is part of a line. It has one endpoint and goes on forever in the other direction. It is named by its endpoint first and one other point. This ray is $\overrightarrow{AB}$.

Name each ray.

1. 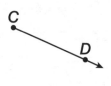   2.   3.    4.

_____   _____   _____   _____

An **angle** is formed by two rays with the same endpoint. The common endpoint is the **vertex** of the angle. An angle can be named three ways.

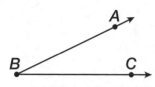 This angle is $\angle ABC$, $\angle CBA$, or $\angle B$. The vertex is named in the middle or alone.

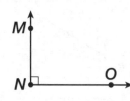 $\angle MNO$ is a right angle. It has a square corner.

Name each angle three ways. If it is a right angle, circle it.

5.   6. 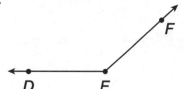   7.

_____   _____   _____

8. 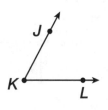   9. 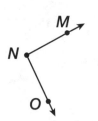   10.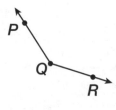

_____   _____   _____

11. 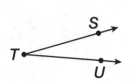   12. 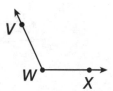   13.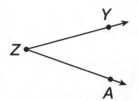

_____   _____   _____

102   Geometry: Rays and Angles

A **polygon** is a plane figure made of line segments called **sides**. The sides meet at points called **vertices**. A polygon is named for the number of sides it has.

| triangle | quadrilateral | pentagon | hexagon | octagon |

Write the number of sides and vertices each polygon has.

1. triangle
   sides ____
   vertices ____

2. quadrilateral
   sides ____
   vertices ____

3. pentagon
   sides ____
   vertices ____

4. hexagon
   sides ____
   vertices ____

5. octagon
   sides ____
   vertices ____

Some **quadrilaterals** have special names.

 A **rectangle** is a quadrilateral with four right angles. The opposite sides are always the same length.

 A **square** is a rectangle with four sides of the same length.

Write *quadrilateral*, *rectangle*, or *square* to name each polygon exactly.

6. _____

7. 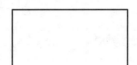 _____

8.  _____

9. 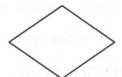 _____

List each part of the sculpture that is—

10. a triangle _____
11. a quadrilateral _____
12. a square _____
13. a rectangle _____
14. a pentagon _____
15. a hexagon _____
16. an octagon _____

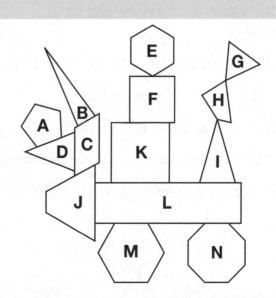

Geometry: Polygons

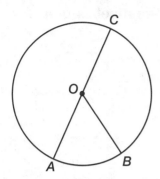

A **circle** is another kind of plane figure. All points on a circle are the same distance from the center.

A **radius** of a circle is a line segment from the center to any point on the circle. $\overline{OB}$, $\overline{OA}$, and $\overline{CO}$ are **radii** of this circle.

A **diameter** of a circle is a line segment that connects two points on a circle and passes through the center. A diameter is always twice as long as a radius. $\overline{CA}$ is a diameter of this circle.

Write *radius* or *diameter* to name each line segment.

1.    2. 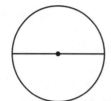   3.    4.

_____   _____   _____   _____

Use this figure to find each answer.

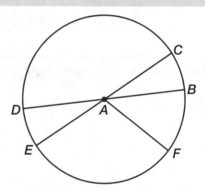

5. Name the center. _____

6. Name three radii. _____

7. Name two diameters. _____

8. If the radius of this circle is 2 miles long, then the diameter is _____ miles long.

Complete.

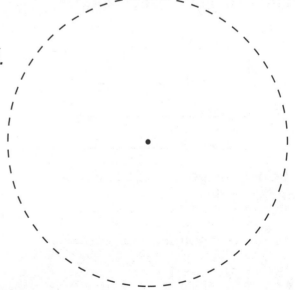

9. Trace the circle on the right and label the center *P*.

10. Draw three radii and label them $\overline{PA}$, $\overline{PB}$, and $\overline{PC}$.

11. Draw a diameter and label it $\overline{DE}$.

12. If a radius of this circle is 6 yards long, then a diameter of it is _____ yards long.

13. If a diameter is 20 feet long, then a radius is _____ feet long.

Congruent polygons have the same shape and the same size.

Similar polygons have the same shape but the sizes may differ.

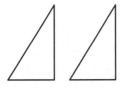 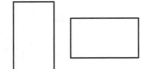 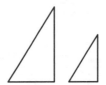 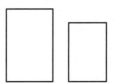

congruent triangles • congruent rectangles • similar triangles • similar rectangles

Write *congruent* or *similar* to describe each pair of figures.

1.
2.
3.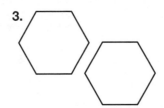
4.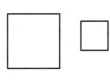

_____ _____ _____ _____

5.
6.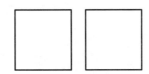
7.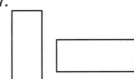
8.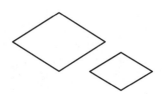

_____ _____ _____ _____

Complete.

9. Name two congruent rectangles.
   _____

10. Name two similar rectangles.
    _____

11. Name two congruent triangles.
    _____

12. Name two similar triangles.
    _____

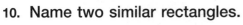
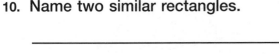
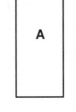

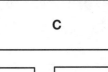
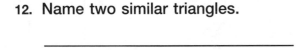
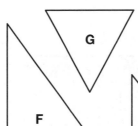
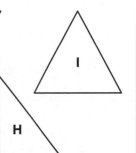

Geometry: Congruence and Similarity

A **symmetrical** figure can be folded along a **line of symmetry** into matching halves.

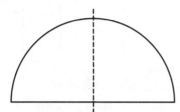

Some figures have more than one line of symmetry.

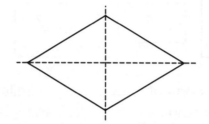

Other figures have no lines of symmetry.

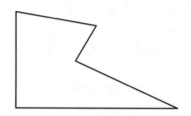

Decide if each figure is symmetrical. Write *yes* or *no* under it.

1.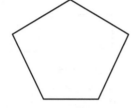
2.
3.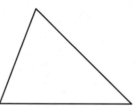
4.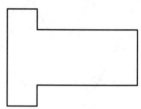

5.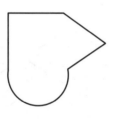
6.
7.
8.

Draw at least one line of symmetry through each figure.

9.
10.
11.
12.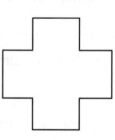

13.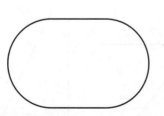
14.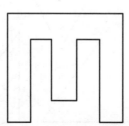
15.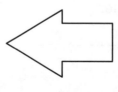
16.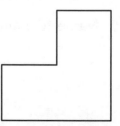

Geometry: Symmetry

An **ordered pair** of numbers names a point on a **grid**.

The first number tells how many units to the right the point is. The second number tells how many units up the point is.

The ordered pair (2, 3) names point A, which is 2 spaces to the right and 3 spaces up.

Point B is (4, 1), and point C is (5, 5).

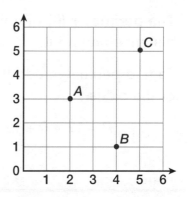

Name the ordered pair for each place.

1. bookstore _____
2. Chinese restaurant _____
3. card shop _____
4. music store _____
5. computer store _____
6. newsstand _____
7. fountain _____
8. pizza shop _____
9. cheese shop _____
10. camera shop _____

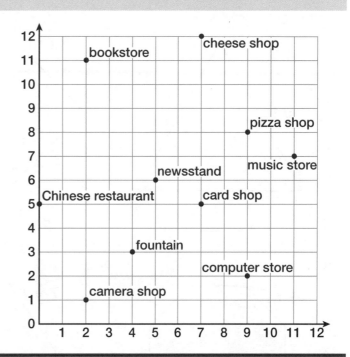

Name the point for each ordered pair.

11. (7, 12) _____
12. (3, 0) _____
13. (2, 2) _____
14. (6, 4) _____
15. (4, 6) _____
16. (12, 7) _____
17. (8, 7) _____
18. (0, 3) _____
19. (10, 9) _____
20. (1, 9) _____

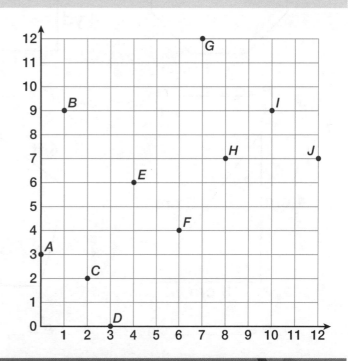

Geometry: Ordered Pairs

107

© The Continental Press, Inc.   DUPLICATING THIS MATERIAL IS ILLEGAL.

The **perimeter** (*P*) of a figure is the distance around it.

To find perimeter, add the lengths of the sides.

P = 12 + 6 + 12 + 6 = 36 meters

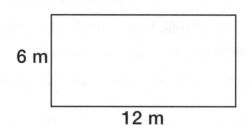

Find the perimeter of each figure.

1.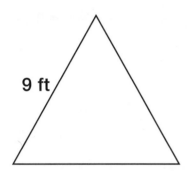

   P = _____ ft

2.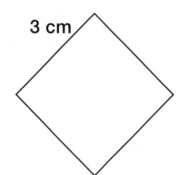

   P = _____ cm

3.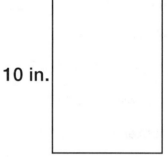

   P = _____ in.

4.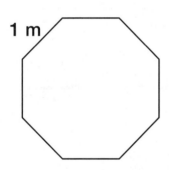

   P = _____ m

5.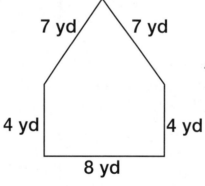

   P = _____ yd

6.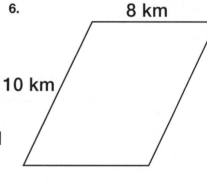

   P = _____ km

7.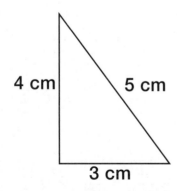

   P = _____ cm

8.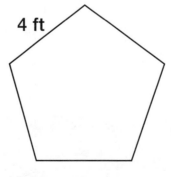

   P = _____ ft

9.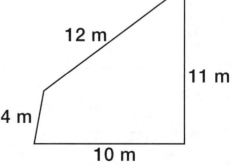

   P = _____ m

Geometry: Perimeter

The **area** (A) of a figure is the number of square units it contains.

To find area, count the square units.

If the figure is a rectangle, you can also multiply the length times the width to find the area.

$$A = 5 \times 3 = 15 \text{ cm}^2$$

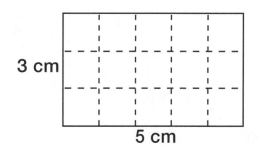

Count to find the area of each figure.

1.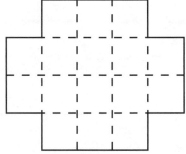

   A = _____ cm²

2.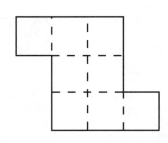

   A = _____ cm²

3.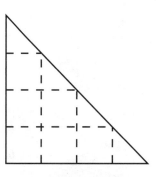

   A = _____ cm²

Multiply to find the area of each figure.

4.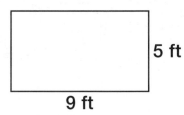

   A = _____ ft²

5.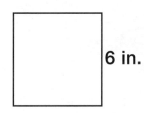

   A = _____ in.²

6.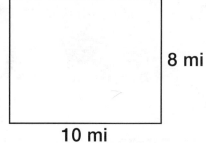

   A = _____ mi²

7.

   A = _____ m²

8.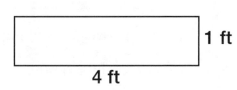

   A = _____ ft²

9.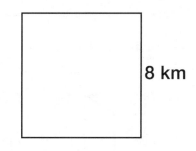

   A = _____ km²

Geometry: Area

Solid geometric figures have special names.

cube   rectangular prism   pyramid   cone   cylinder   sphere

Name each shape.

1.
_____

2.
_____

3.
_____

4.
_____

5.
_____

6.
_____

7.
_____

8.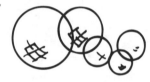
_____

9.
_____

10.
_____

11.
_____

12.
_____

Complete.

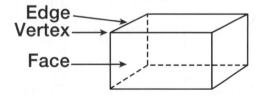

Edge, Vertex, Face

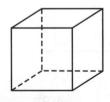 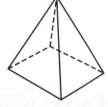

13. A rectangular prism has _____ vertices, _____ faces, and _____ edges.

14. A square pyramid has _____ vertices, _____ faces, and _____ edges.

15. A cube has _____ vertices, _____ faces, and _____ edges.

110   Geometry: Solid Figures

The **volume** (V) of a figure is the number of **cubic units** it contains.

To find volume, count the cubic units.

If the figure is a rectangular prism or a cube, you can also multiply the length times the width times the height to find the volume.

$$V = 3 \times 2 \times 2 = 12 \text{ cm}^3$$

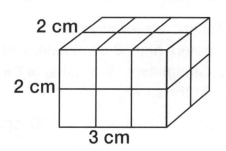

Count to find the volume of each figure.

1.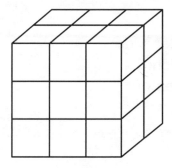

   V = _____ cm³

2.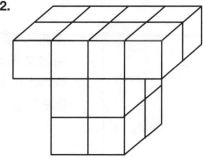

   V = _____ cm³

3.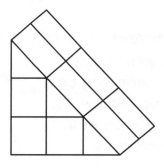

   V = _____ cm³

Multiply to find the volume of each figure.

4.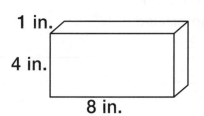

   V = _____ in.³

5.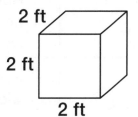

   V = _____ ft³

6.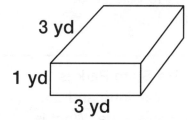

   V = _____ yd³

7.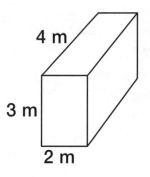

   V = _____ m³

8.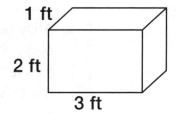

   V = _____ ft³

9.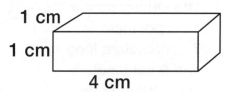

   V = _____ cm³

Geometry: Volume

Drawing a picture can help you solve some problems.

Mrs. Nishimoto's jewelry box is 5 centimeters high, 8 centimeters wide, and 12 centimeters long. What is the volume of the box?

$V = 5 \times 8 \times 12 = 480$ cm³

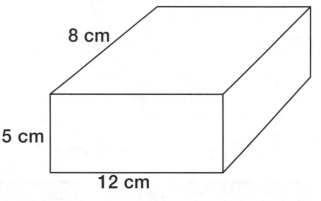

Draw a picture to help you solve each problem.

1. Mr. Austen's garden is a square that is 9 yards long on a side. What is the perimeter of the garden?

2. A flag is 1 meter wide and 2 meters long. What is the area of the flag?

3. Monica's horse trailer is 1 meter wide, 2 meters high, and 3 meters long. What is the volume of the trailer?

4. The Rocking R Ranch is a rectangle that is 15 kilometers long and 8 kilometers wide. How much fencing is needed to go around its perimeter?

5. Pike State Park is 7 miles long and 4 miles wide. What is the area of the park?

6. Kurt's room is 3 yards wide, 4 yards long, and 3 yards high. What is the volume of Kurt's room?

7. The writing space on a postcard is 7 centimeters long and 6 centimeters wide. What is the area of the writing space?

8. A lily pond is 2 feet deep, 6 feet wide, and 9 feet long. What is the volume of the lily pond?

Multiplying by tens is like multiplying by ones.

```
   58        58
   ×2       ×20
  116     1,160
```

Think of 20 × 58 as 2 × 10 × 58.
Write a 0 in the ones place of the product.
Then multiply by 2.

Multiply.

1. 43 × 30
2. 74 × 10
3. 21 × 80
4. 65 × 40
5. 27 × 60

6. 18 × 70
7. 89 × 50
8. 32 × 90
9. 56 × 20
10. 92 × 30

11. 882 × 10
12. 173 × 20
13. 265 × 80
14. 436 × 40
15. 649 × 50

16. $2.08 × 50
17. $8.70 × 30
18. $5.74 × 70
19. $4.83 × 60
20. $1.56 × 90

21. The Longs used 50 gallons of gas on a vacation trip. If their car gets 30 miles to the gallon, how many miles did they travel?

22. The Longs used 20 gallons of gas the first day. If gas cost $2.20 a gallon, how much did gas cost in all the first day?

Multiplying by Tens

113

```
   63    Think of 28 as 20 + 8.
  ×28    Multiply by the ones: 8 × 63 = 504.
  504    Multiply by the tens: 20 × 63 = 1,260.
 1260    Add the products: 504 + 1,260 = 1,764.
1,764
```

Multiply.

1. 81
   ×16 (10 + 6)

2. 54
   ×72 (70 + 2)

3. 19
   ×82 (80 + 2)

4. 97
   ×43

5. 75
   ×27

6. 83
   ×36

7. 58
   ×48

8. 39
   ×64

9. 27
   ×51

10. 69
   ×45

11. 41
   ×93

12. 14
   ×78

13. 76
   ×56

14. 32
   ×23

15. Carolyn unpacked 19 cartons of cereal. Each carton held 12 boxes of cereal. How many boxes did Carolyn unpack?

16. There are 36 cans of beans in a case. Carolyn opened 21 cases and put the cans on the shelves. How many cans is that?

114   Multiplying by Two-Digit Numbers

$$\begin{array}{r}254\\ \times 36\\\hline 1524\\ 7620\\\hline 9{,}144\end{array}$$

Think of 36 as 30 + 6.
Multiply by the ones: 6 × 254 = 1,524.
Multiply by the tens: 30 × 254 = 7,620.
Add the products: 1,524 + 7,620 = 9,144.

Multiply.

1. 185 × 42
2. 940 × 71
3. 408 × 65
4. 762 × 19

5. 317 × 93
6. 196 × 84
7. 823 × 55
8. 546 × 39

9. 628 × 76
10. 914 × 25
11. 256 × 83
12. 712 × 49

Find each answer above in the code box. Then write the matching letters in the spaces below to solve the riddle.

Why is it hard to talk with a goat around?

__ __ __ __ __ __ __   __ __
4 11 6 1 7 5 11   8 12

__ __ __ __ __ __
1 10 9 1 2 5

__ __ __ __ __   __ __
4 7 12 12 5   8 3

CODE
7,770 = A
14,478 = B
16,464 = C
21,248 = E
21,294 = I
22,850 = L
26,520 = N
29,481 = S
34,888 = T
45,265 = U
47,728 = W
66,740 = Y

Multiplying by Two-Digit Numbers

Dividing by tens is easy. Look at these examples.

$$3\overline{)6}=2 \qquad 30\overline{)60}=2 \qquad 30\overline{)65}=2\ R5 \qquad 4\overline{)16}=4 \qquad 40\overline{)160}=4 \qquad 40\overline{)170}=4\ R10$$

Check your answer by multiplying. Add any remainder.

Divide. Check by multiplying. Remember to add a remainder.

1. $20\overline{)60}$
2. $40\overline{)82}$
3. $30\overline{)90}$
4. $20\overline{)80}$

5. $80\overline{)160}$
6. $50\overline{)251}$
7. $60\overline{)300}$
8. $70\overline{)210}$

9. $40\overline{)369}$
10. $90\overline{)456}$
11. $70\overline{)562}$
12. $80\overline{)640}$

13. $60\overline{)427}$
14. $30\overline{)282}$
15. $90\overline{)825}$
16. $50\overline{)400}$

17. How many buses are needed for 320 people if 40 people can ride on a bus?

18. Ace Printers packed 450 invitations into bundles of 50. How many bundles were there?

Dividing by Tens

To divide by tens and ones, round the divisor to the nearest ten and estimate.

$$\begin{array}{r} 9 \text{ R15} \\ 49\overline{)456} \\ \underline{441} \\ 15 \end{array}$$

49 is about 50.
456 ÷ 50 is about 9.
Because 9 × 50 = 450.
Write 9 in the **ones** place.
Multiply: 9 × 49 = 441.
Subtract: 456 − 441 = 15.
15 is the remainder.

Divide. Check by multiplying. Remember to add any remainder.

1. $41\overline{)287}$ Think: 287 ÷ 40 is about 7
   $\underline{287}$

2. $28\overline{)240}$ Think: 240 ÷ 30

3. $84\overline{)504}$ Think: 504 ÷ 80

4. $63\overline{)189}$

5. $45\overline{)300}$

6. $19\overline{)181}$

7. $92\overline{)460}$

8. $34\overline{)239}$

9. $57\overline{)480}$

10. $81\overline{)330}$

11. $62\overline{)496}$

12. $23\overline{)207}$

13. $38\overline{)367}$

14. $79\overline{)405}$

15. $54\overline{)324}$

16. Zhu has 738 CDs. If he stores 82 CDs on a shelf, how many shelves are filled?

17. Zhu burnt 176 songs onto CDs. If he put 22 songs on each CD, how many did he fill?

Dividing by Two-Digit Numbers

Sometimes the quotient is a two-digit number.

```
      42
21 ) 882
     84
     42
     42
```

21 is about 20. Since 10 × 20 = 200, the quotient is a two-digit number.
First, find the tens. 882 has 88 tens, so divide 88: 88 ÷ 20 is about 4.
Write 4 in the **tens** place.
Multiply: 4 × 21 = 84. Subtract 88 − 84 = 4.
Bring down the ones.
Now find the ones: 42 ÷ 20 is about 2.
Multiply: 2 × 21 = 42. Subtract: 42 − 42 = 0.

Divide. Check by multiplying.

1. 58) 696 Think: 69 ÷ 60
2. 83) 913 Think: 91 ÷ 80
3. 48) 624 Think: 62 ÷ 50

4. 32) 960
5. 28) 700
6. 42) 672
7. 63) 945

8. 41) 861
9. 27) 729
10. 39) 663
11. 22) 506

12. Tricksey's Fun Shop ordered 504 masks for Halloween. They came in boxes of 42 masks. How many boxes was that?

13. Tricksey's ordered 550 costumes in 22 styles. The same number of each style was ordered. How many of each style were ordered?

Dividing by Two-Digit Numbers

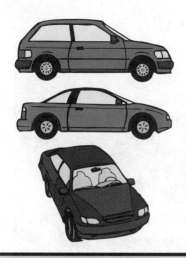

MODEL OF CAR	GALLONS OF GAS TANK HOLDS	MILES PER GALLON	
		City Driving	Highway Driving
Excel Standard	14	25	42
Excel Plus	18	23	37
Excel Master	20	19	28
Excel Super	23	18	25
Excel Luxury	25	17	23

Use the information in the chart to help you solve each problem. Check your answers.

1. Mrs. Donelly has an Excel Luxury. How many miles can she drive on the highway on a full tank of gas?

2. Mr. Smith drove 380 miles in the city this week. His car is an Excel Master. How many gallons of gas did he use?

3. Darcy drives her Excel Standard 325 miles each week to work in city traffic. How many gallons of gas does she use each week?

4. Kazim has an Excel Plus. How much does it cost to fill up its gas tank if gas costs $2.45 a gallon?

5. Ms. Sanchez has an Excel Super. How many miles can she drive in the city on a full tank of gas?

6. Bob is 97 miles away on highways. Shelley has 3 gallons of gas in her Excel Standard. Must she buy gas to get to Bob?

7. Timber Lake is 610 miles away on highways. The Becks have an Excel Plus. Can they get to the lake on one tank of gas?

8. Mrs. Wang drove 228 miles in the city, using 12 gallons of gas. How many miles per gallon did she get? What kind of car did she drive?

Problem Solving: Using Rates

Some problems can be solved by guessing the answer and checking it.

The 24 horses on the Big Sky Ranch are either black or brown. There are 6 more brown horses than black horses. How many horses are there of each color?

Guess 9 for the number of black horses. If there are 9 black horses, then the number of brown horses is 9 + 6, or 15.
Check: 9 + 15 = 24.

So there are 9 black horses and 15 brown ones.

Make a guess and check it to solve each problem.

1. The sum of the numbers of cats and dogs that live on the ranch is 14. The product of the numbers is 45. There are more cats than dogs. How many of each kind of animal live on the ranch?

2. Selma's dad is 4 times as old as she is. The sum of their ages is 60. How old are Selma and her dad?

3. Two pastures have a total area of 96 acres. One pasture is twice as big as the other. What is the area of each pasture?

4. Chris and his mom loaded 38 bales of hay onto a truck. Chris loaded 6 fewer bales than his mom did. How many bales of hay did each person load?

Problem Solving: Guessing and Checking